"Barb Roose's *Stronger than Stress* [...] an overwhelming world, offering [...] tual practices. As an advocate for [...] her insights into stress triggers, emphasizing the creation of lasting strength. This book, rooted in Jesus-centered, grace-based tools, is a must-read for those seeking resilience, deeper connection, and a purposeful, peaceful life."

Lucretia Carter Berry, PhD, visionary founder of Brownicity, offering education that brings us together

"In *Stronger than Stress*, Roose beckons us to reckon with our stress and its hold on our lives as we envision a new way forward, one of wholeness and peace, goodness and truth. Her honesty reminds us that life is hard for everyone, and with practices to renew us, we'll be able to handle life's blows, come what may."

Tiffany Bluhm, author of *Prey Tell*

"If you're tired of living at the mercy of circumstance and in survival mode and instead want to experience a fresh infusion of strength, do yourself a favor: add Barb Roose's voice of wisdom to your current reality. Through the pages of her book *Stronger than Stress*, Barb offers counsel that is both empowering and practical, giving you insight into the why behind your actions and reactions and then delivering powerful strategies to successfully navigate uncertainty. She's a resource you don't want to live without."

Michele Cushatt, author of *A Faith That Will Not Fail*

"If 'overwhelmed' is how you describe your life more often than you would care to admit, you need this book. With openness and warmth, Barb Roose is the friend who has been there too, and the guide you need who graciously paves the way back to biblical truth that transforms step-by-step. When peace seems hard to come by, *Stronger than Stress* will be your go-to resource to help you overcome your overwhelm."

Ashley Morgan Jackson, speaker and writer for Proverbs 31 Ministries and bestselling author of *Tired of Trying*

"Barb normalizes how common and even rampant overwhelm is, especially in the lives of women. This book gave me a set of glasses to identify my overwhelm that has been bubbling under my surface, and it provides practical tools and solutions. Spinning plates, decision fatigue, the pace of life, uncertainty, and stress starters all lead to magnifying our overwhelmed state. Barb writes with vulnerability, authenticity, and humor on how to tackle stress from a biblical perspective. She includes breathing exercises, mindset adjustments, and self-awareness clues to help us reorient ourselves to God and away from our initial stress responses. Her use of sticky phrases and acronyms like QTIP (Quit Taking It Personally) are powerful tools to learn and let this message linger during times of stress when this book isn't in your hands. Grab it for yourself, and grab a few extras for the special women in your life who are trying to do it all."

Lisa J. Allen, board-certified confidence coach and speaker, L. J. Allen Coaching

"In *Stronger than Stress*, Roose masterfully combines biblical wisdom with relatable narratives, guiding readers through the labyrinth of life's stresses with grace and strength. Filled with tangible tools that are easily put into practice, this is a must-read for those on the path to spiritual and emotional resilience."

Heather M. Dixon, national speaker and author of *Determined*

"If stress and overwhelm feel like a prison you're chronically doomed to occupy, you need Barb Roose's new book. *Stronger than Stress* breaks down the stigma and shame of living in a state of overwhelm and assures readers that their faith isn't false for feeling stressed-out. Rather, Barb uses biblical truths, scientific facts, and her personal experience to shed light on the root causes of stress so we can overcome our overwhelm today, tomorrow, and always. No trite platitudes in these pages. Just a trusted Bible teacher and honest friend who has won the battle and wants to see you win too."

Becky Keife, author of *Create in Me a Heart of Peace* and *The Simple Difference*

"Barb Roose is a ride-or-die friend and trusted mentor who helps us understand and navigate the complexities of stress. This book is the perfect integration of humor, theology, brain science, and relatable storytelling."

Dorina Lazo Gilmore-Young, award-winning author, speaker, and Bible teacher

STRONGER *than stress*

STRONGER
than stress

10 SPIRITUAL PRACTICES TO WIN
THE BATTLE OF OVERWHELM

BARB ROOSE

Revell

a division of Baker Publishing Group
Grand Rapids, Michigan

Published by Revell
a division of Baker Publishing Group
Grand Rapids, Michigan
RevellBooks.com

Printed in the United States of America

Library of Congress Cataloging-in-Publication Data
Names: Roose, Barbara L., author.
Title: Stronger than stress : 10 spiritual practices to win the battle of overwhelm / Barb Roose.
Description: Grand Rapids, Michigan : Revell, a division of Baker Publishing Group, 2024. | Includes bibliographical references.
Identifiers: LCCN 2023056483 | ISBN 9780800744915 (paper) | ISBN 9780800745936 (casebound) | ISBN 9781493445608 (ebook)
Subjects: LCSH: Worry—Religious aspects—Christianity. | Stress management—Religious aspects—Christianity. | Spiritual life—Christianity.
Classification: LCC BV4908.5 .R583 2024 | DDC 248.8/6—dc23/eng/20240206
LC record available at https://lccn.loc.gov/2023056483

Unless otherwise indicated, Scripture quotations are from the *Holy Bible*, New Living Translation. Copyright © 1996, 2004, 2015 by Tyndale House Foundation. Used by permission of Tyndale House Publishers, Carol Stream, Illinois 60188. All rights reserved.

Scripture quotations labeled MSG are from *The Message*. Copyright © 1993, 2002, 2018 by Eugene H. Peterson. Used by permission of NavPress. All rights reserved. Represented by Tyndale House Publishers.

Italics added to Scripture quotations reflect the author's emphasis.

This publication is intended to provide helpful and informative material on the subjects addressed. Readers should consult their personal health professionals before adopting any of the suggestions in this book or drawing inferences from it. The author and publisher expressly disclaim responsibility for any adverse effects arising from the use or application of the information contained in this book.

Cover design by Mumtaz Mustafa Design

Published in association with Books & Such Literary Management, www.BooksAndSuch.com.

Baker Publishing Group publications use paper produced from sustainable forestry practices and postconsumer waste whenever possible.

24 25 26 27 28 29 30   7 6 5 4 3 2 1

To my text thread besties,
my Fab Five Sisters,
my McDonald's coffee date,
my Flying Jo partner,
my DC heart,
my Mr. Freeze Mama,
my Adventure Ami,
and my Red Lobster ride or die . . .

You are the beautiful evidence
of God's great and unconditional love for me
in seasons of both overwhelm and victory.
I love you and am so grateful for each of you.

CONTENTS

INTRODUCTION

I can't do all of this.
If anything else happens, I'm going to have a stroke.
I just want to cry.
Have you found yourself thinking things like this lately? Or
do you hear yourself uttering these words more often?

None of us want to live this way. Living stressed-out is exhausting and discouraging. When we're overwhelmed, that
overflows into complicating our relationships with others and
lowers our capacity to take care of ourselves. This isn't the life
that we want.

If this describes what you've experienced lately, I'm glad that
you're here. If you're overwhelmed, that's understandable, but
with God's strength it is totally possible to overcome your daily
stress and experience peace.

I know this about you: you are doing the very best you can
in a life where you have too much to do, too little time to do it,
while trying not to mess up. You're showing up with the best
fight that you've got, but it's hard to hang in there. Your life
looks like endless spinning plates. You want to keep up, but
you've had too little sleep, you're stretched too thin, and there's
not enough coffee in the world to help you get it all done. None

of us want to spend our lives trying to hold everything around us together but feeling like we're always about to fall apart. What would it mean for our lives to be different?

For decades, I believed that stress and overwhelm were normal. I'd been successful in my careers in the marketplace and ministry. Awards hung on the wall and I'd accomplished so many worthwhile goals, but the cost was constant exhaustion, inability to be present with my family, and a deep desire to escape from my life. However, I didn't think that my struggle was unique. Most people around me were stressed-out, so I never questioned whether there was another path.

During one of my seasons of burnout, I joined a yearlong women's leadership discipleship group at my church. It was there that I first learned about spiritual practices. We called them spiritual disciplines back then, but for me, that experience was a game changer in my ability to open myself up to connecting with God better. Instead of insisting that I had to be in charge and figure everything out, which was stressful, these practices taught me how to slow down, savor, and find safety in the security of God's love and grace and the transforming power of the Holy Spirit.

I invite you on a journey so that God can do the same for you as He did for me.

As a Christian women's speaker and author, I've heard from thousands of women over the years, and there are unique stresses, areas of overwhelm, and discipleship struggles that so many of us share in common. I decided that I'd combine what I've learned about spiritual practices over the years with my experience as a Bible teacher, leader, and pharmaceutical sales representative to offer hope to women that God has given us— you—everything that we need to win the battle of overwhelm.

Our guide for this journey will be the apostle Paul. He was a first-century pastor, church planter, and prolific writer of many New Testament letters, and most notably, Paul considered himself a humble follower of Jesus Christ. Paul faced angry mobs, relational conflict, shipwrecks, physical threats, beatings, imprisonment, and court cases. What's wild is that those stressful circumstances came *after* he began following Jesus.

Paul is honest about life's challenging circumstances, but still, he intentionally calls us to have greater devotion and faith in Christ. We'll learn about how to do this from his example, his teachings, and his story. Additional benefits you will experience include:

- Learn the four main stress triggers that push you toward the breaking point and how to anticipate them in advance.
- Discover the power of what I call "Breathing Room" exercises to help you interrupt your fight-or-flight stress response and prepare you to engage in the spiritual practices.
- Stop living in survival mode and learn how to practice God's peace.
- Cultivate your knowledge of the ten spiritual practices that create space for you to connect intimately with God, giving Him space to transform you from overwhelmed to overcomer no matter what you're facing in life.
- Learn practical, Scripture-based tools and how to apply them to your daily life in a Jesus-centered, grace-based way.
- Wake up with daily confidence that you can live at peace and in wholeness even though you may be living in difficult or stressful circumstances.

This is a journey that will require you to trust that God can do what you can't in winning your battle of overwhelm. If you are willing, God will work in your heart, mind, and life. The beautiful truth about your healing is that it is already waiting for you because it has already been won. Jesus already accomplished this victory for you. It's waiting if you are willing. Winning the battle of overwhelm looks like living with a calm heart and a peaceful mind. As a result, you live from the power of God's peace so that you can participate in God's eternal purpose.

I'm glad that you're joining me for this journey!

1

GIVE ME A BREAK

It's okay to not be okay.

Barb Roose

I didn't realize that I'd thrown those dinner plates through my kitchen window until the sound of shattered glass snapped me back into reality. Even before I fully surveyed the glass and porcelain carnage, my mind's public relations office worked to spin the disaster: *Ohhhh, that's not good. Yikes, you can't walk that back, honey. Think. How do we explain this without admitting what really happened? Can you tell your neighbors that those plates just happened to slip out of your hands?*

Those plates did not slip out of my hands, unless slipping looks a lot like Nolan Ryan firing off a fastball from the pitching mound. When I opened the back door to what looked like a crime scene after a home robbery, I realized I had tossed more than a few plates. I'd also fired off several forks, a mixing bowl, my salad colander, and a classic white Corelle coffee mug, which blessedly honored its no-break guarantee. At least there was that.

While that mug didn't break, it was time to admit that I finally had.

My overwhelm had overcome me. It had broken me. It wasn't the first time. This was just the messiest, most embarrassing time.

I raced up the steps and threw myself on the loveseat in my TV room. My cheeks flamed with the shame of failure. I never thought that I'd go over the edge like that, but I should have known. Parenting, work, household, grief, a loved one's addiction, car troubles, struggling kids. Again, I should have known.

Ohhh, the neighbors... My cheeks warmed again from embarrassment. I made it clear to everyone around me that I was a Christian. They knew that I worked for my church. Christian women aren't supposed to throw plates through their kitchen window. *What have I done? God, did I totally embarrass You?* Like Adam and Eve in the garden, I wanted to hide. I knew that God loved me, but if I were Him, I'd be disappointed in me for losing all self-control in a most spectacular way.

The heaviness followed me back downstairs to revisit the scene of the crime. Tears fell as I swept up the evidence of my stressed-out life. I sagged against the wall as I reclimbed the steps to cry on the loveseat again. I'd cleaned up the mess, but I had no idea how to clean up the mess that had become my life.

God, I'm overwhelmed and I don't know what to do.

What Is Overwhelm?

I begin our journey together by telling my story so that if you're wondering how your life became so hard, complicated, and confusing, you'll know you're not alone. It's so hard waking up and knowing that you're doing the best that you can when it feels like you're falling further behind and falling apart more every day.

A common dictionary description of overwhelm is a sensation of being buried or drowning, feeling defeated, and being unable to know what to do next.[1] But here is my practical definition of overwhelm: *having too much to do with not enough time to do it, and feeling unsure, paralyzed, or stuck on how to fix it or move forward.*

Overwhelm is something that we sense before we can name it. I can be busy and doing just fine, but then I remember that I need to transfer money from one bank to the next before 5 p.m. That requires a phone call and waiting indefinitely for customer service. I don't have time for that. I also need to pick up a prescription at some point between my three Zoom calls. I should have transferred the money a week ago, so I beat myself up for procrastinating. One of those Zoom calls is about a problem that someone is depending on me to solve, but I don't have the answers. While I'm sorting through all that and attempting to fill in my right eyebrow (which never turns out as good as my left eyebrow), one of the kids asks to borrow my car. I stare at myself in the bathroom mirror.

Then, I feel it. The start of a pit in the middle of my stomach. Two words come to mind: *Oh no.*

This is overwhelm.

It's complex. It's a chaos of details, emotions, and overload that demands your attention, but you don't know what to do with it. The inability to sort out your overwhelm terrifies you because so much is at stake in your life. You can't afford to mess things up, and you've got to figure it out before it's too late.

My hope is to meet you in that space with the love of Christ and the guiding light of God's truth. Deep breath, my friend. If God led you to these pages, then He knows how to take care of you and handle things while you sort through your overwhelm.

I've been there. A few times. There is a path to the other side of your overwhelm. What you'll learn here will not only give insight into what's going on inside you but will help you know how to stop the spinning, grab God's hand, and let Him lead you to the other side where you can experience His peace, joy, and victory.

Overwhelm as an Internal Emotion

Overwhelm is a mixture of emotions and experiences, but there are no precise measurements. The recipe for overwhelm is a pinch of this and a "teense" of that (a Southern way of saying tiny or teensy). It's not precise, but it's accurate nonetheless, like my grandmother's way of cooking intuitively without a recipe.

To help you remember the elements of overwhelm, I developed the acronym CATS, which is funny for me because I am a dog person. When it comes to overwhelm, CATS stands for *control, anxiety, time,* and *stress.* For my own life, when that pit starts in my stomach, I ask myself which of these are in play. You can use this as a diagnostic tool in your battle to help you identify overwhelm in the future.

C—Control

- **Too Little Control: One's inability to manage or change the situation**

Your ability to manage or change the situation is an important factor in the extent to which you'll experience overwhelm. The less control that you have or feel like you have, the easier it will be for you to feel overwhelmed.

If all four tires on your car need to be replaced and you have the money in your account, this will likely cause annoyance for an out-of-service car, but not overwhelm. But if you're already behind on your bills, your mind may start spinning on not only the repair bill but how you will handle the other bills. That will spark worries about taking care of yourself and others.

There's also a hidden layer within the level of control. I've heard it described as *active challenge* and *passive challenge*.[2] Active challenges are the complex circumstances you choose to pursue, such as going back to college, building a house, or starting a business. When you say yes to those opportunities and the pressure builds, you can still feel overwhelmed, but you are likely to be more positive and hopeful toward your overwhelm because you agreed to it. Passive challenges are circumstances that are thrust on you and you had no say in them, whether it's having parents who struggled with addiction, a spouse's infidelity, a job layoff, or a health crisis. This form of overwhelm can create more distress and hopelessness since you had no choice in the matter but are left to find your path through it.

A—Anxiety

- **Too Much Anxiety: Fear for your safety or fear of the unknown**

This is the emotion that we associate most often with overwhelm. Anxiety describes both our state of mind and our emotional reaction. It's also how we describe our undefined fears. Anxiety asks questions like "Will I be okay?" or "What if something bad happens to me?" or "Can someone tell me what will happen?"

There are two parts to anxiety: physical and mental. Physical expressions of anxiety include a racing heartbeat, sleeplessness, nausea, upset stomach, anger, shaky hands, irritability, or frequent crying. The mental layer of anxiety is worry. This includes overthinking, distraction, or fixating on worst-case scenarios, which I call WorryFlix.[3]

If you lost your job but had six months of savings in your checking account, you'd be less likely to move toward overwhelm. You'd feel some level of safety and security in knowing that you'd have a roof over your head and food to eat. In another example, if the doctor diagnoses you with a chronic illness and advises you to change jobs, the questions about your quality of life and ability to provide for yourself would understandably generate anxiety that would contribute to overwhelm.

T—Time

- **Too Little Time: Not enough hours and minutes to accomplish tasks**

Raise your hand if you tend to be overly optimistic about what you can accomplish on any given day. Both of my hands are up.

Buses, trains, and airlines run on a schedule. Our lives do not, but we live like they do and we're always up against a clock. It's like the music to Final Jeopardy plays in our minds all the time. We need to make a move, make a decision, make it to an appointment, or make something right, but there never seems to be enough time.

Unfortunately, we don't do ourselves any favors by not accounting for the inevitable time sinks such as having an extra-slow cashier at the grocery store, waiting on others, forgetting to put gas in the car, or the baby having a blowout diaper before we leave the house.

When you don't have enough time and then you lose control over the time that you do have—well, that's a big push toward overwhelm.

S—Stress

- **Too Much Stress: Anything that you perceive as threatening or adding pressure to your life.**

Stress is the body's internal response to external pressure. In the next chapter, we're going to break down stress because it's an important player in overwhelm. When stress is sustained for too long, our bodies will swing toward overwhelm because there's a sense that something has been going wrong for a long time and we haven't been able to fix it.

CATS is a description of the factors of overwhelm. However, I did not address certain conditions like trauma, mental health disorders, chronic illness, and grief. These are important factors that can predispose one to overwhelm, accelerate overwhelm, or make it difficult to treat. If you know that one of these conditions is contributing to and increasing your overwhelm or is making it difficult for you to concentrate on the spiritual practices discussed in this book, then this is where I highly recommend having a mental health professional join you in this journey.

Overwhelm's External Battle

We've looked at what creates overwhelm inside of us, but overwhelm is also an experience made up of our circumstances and environments.

If I had to create a word picture for overwhelm, it looks like a room of spinning plates. We all have a unique set of spinning plates. My spinning plates look like an 84-piece set of beautifully, individually painted Polish pottery. A sweet friend gave me a Polish pottery mug for Christmas one year and I fell in love with the style.

My spinning plates come in all shapes and sizes. Each size represents some part of my life.

The little saucers are my to-do list items. There's a spinning saucer for filing my business receipts. Another saucer spins and reminds me to put gas in my car at night instead of waiting until the morning. Not all the spinning plates are task oriented. Fun plates include invitations to lunch, time with special people, or adventurous plans.

Next up are salad plates, which are the unresolved but important issues in my life like finding a new dentist, setting up a meeting with my financial planner, or deciding whether to buy or lease a car. My daughter's car required extensive repairs after a weird auto accident involving a tree stump that fell off a landscape truck. Eight weeks later, the repair shop called to tell us that her seat belt needed to be replaced and there were no seat belts in the country to match her vehicle. I hoped that plate could come down, but it continued to spin for many more months.

The dinner plates symbolize my relationships. I love those plates, but they hold a lot of drama and complicated dynamics, so they wobble real easily. I can't blame the plates because I'm also heaping my expectations and desires on top like extra gravy. Those plates take a lot of effort to spin. Whew. I'm tired just thinking about it.

Finally, there are the serving platters, which represent emergencies or crisis situations such as an unexpected job loss, a health crisis, a financial setback, or even a small problem that you blow up into a crisis because of fear or overthinking. Regardless of how the crisis happens, it requires tremendous energy and effort to keep minding their spinning pole.

What does your spinning plate room look like? If you'd like, grab a sheet of paper and draw each size plate and label them. It might be an eye-opening activity. Once we look at our plates, it's natural to wonder:

- How many plates are too many?
- What if I can't handle the plates that I have?
- Am I a horrible person if I let a plate drop?
- How can I stop other people from adding to my plates?

These are all good questions that I believe God will equip you to discern in our time together. As you learn how God equips us to win the battle of overwhelm, He will provide you with more tools to apply wisdom to what's happening in your life.

Next, I want to go back to the desperate prayer that I cried out to God at the beginning of this chapter.

God, I'm Overwhelmed . . .

God, I'm overwhelmed and I don't know what to do. Have you ever prayed that prayer?

Maybe this is a good time to pause, take a deep breath, and use the words that King David prayed when his son Absalom once plotted to overthrow his kingdom: "Please listen and answer me, for I am *overwhelmed* by my troubles" (Ps. 55:2). David goes on to describe his heart pounding in his chest, and a few verses later he again uses the word *overwhelm*: "Fear and trembling overwhelm me, and I can't stop shaking" (v. 5). He even wishes that he was a bird so that he could fly away.

Overwhelm is nothing to be ashamed of. Life is often more than we can handle, even for someone who has been walking with Jesus for a long time. Spiritual maturity doesn't mean that you won't experience overwhelm, but your connection with God keeps you from getting stuck there.

God has a great adventure of faith and a purpose for each of our lives, so He won't let overwhelm steal your hope, joy, or peace. In the following chapters, you'll learn how to create space for God to step into your stress and grow your character, your patience, and your hope so that you will win the battle of overwhelm as an overcomer!

2

TOO STRESSED TO BE BLESSED

God didn't promise a stress-free life. He promised to give
you the strength to live this life.

Barb Roose

Experiencing overwhelm or stress is not something to hide or a
reason for shame. Nor is experiencing stress a sign of spiritual
immaturity or lack of faith. We all experience stress. If the doctor delivers a type 1 diabetes diagnosis for your ten-year-old,
you'll feel stress. That is normal. If your job gets eliminated,
you may experience stress. If your son leaves the house with
friends but you know that he's headed to a side of town where
someone of his skin color might not be welcome, you may feel
stress. Stress happens.

God sees you and the distress that weighs on your heart.

I prayed to the LORD, and he answered me.
He freed me from all my fears.

> Those who look to him for help will be radiant with joy;
> no shadow of shame will darken their faces. (Ps.
> 34:4–5)

This is one of those passages that I keep close by during seasons of stress when life happens and weariness causes me to wonder if God cares about what I'm going through. He does.

However, living in a constant state of stress or overwhelm is a spiritual red flag, an emotional danger zone, and a physical threat. Red flags aren't judgments or signs that you're doing something wrong. They are indicators that something could be wrong. Prolonged stress can lead to unhealthy or sinful behaviors, as well as cause significant damage to your mental and physical health. Living in chronic stress means that you're living without the healing, sustaining peace that God promises. It prevents you from living out God's great adventure of faith and purpose for your life. Winning your battle against overwhelm isn't only about exchanging your stress for peace; ultimately, this is about finding freedom so that you can experience all that God promises and live out your purpose.

You already know that your stressed life is not your best life. We need to talk about stress because it is a physical and spiritual indicator of what's going on inside you. God cares about what's going on inside you, and He has wired your body to help you take care of yourself.

Why Does God Allow Us to Experience Stress?

There's a common belief that all stress is bad, but that's not true. In its healthy, functional form, stress has a God-ordained protective purpose. Stress is an indication of how you're reacting to the world around you, and it can help you adjust so that you can protect your God-given body from hurt or harm. Think about stress like a red flag. Red flags are indicators, not verdicts.

Why in heaven would God create stress if He knew that it would create so many potential problems? We could ask that same question of why God would create sex, work, parenting, or relationships. Each of those things is good and has divine origins, yet because we live in a world impacted by sin, good things created by God have been perverted by sin, and that breaks God's heart as much as it does yours.

How you handle your stress determines whether you'll experience healthy stress, which protects you from harm or injury, or harmful stress, which can have life-altering consequences, including a number of health issues and even death.

Do you know how stress starts in your body?

There's a network in your body called the autonomic nervous system that scans the world around you, looking for any threat or danger. This system operates without your conscious awareness. Additionally, there is an almond-sized system in your brain called the amygdala. This system is looking for anything that your body interprets as unsafe or that will undermine your security.[1] It identifies patterns in hopes of preventing danger from happening again. The amygdala asks questions like, "Is this something I hate? Will this hurt me? Is this something I fear?"[2]

On an environmental level, your subconscious nervous system scans your surroundings for physical threats like a speeding car or a dog chasing you. Additionally, this system may interpret your reaction to receiving an unexpected tax bill or seeing a questionable text message as possible threats.

If your amygdala picks up on any kind of emotional impulse that you feel unsafe or threatened, it activates a stress response, commonly referred to as the fight-or-flight survival response.

Imagine that a lion appears and starts chasing you with its shiny fangs in full view. Your body reacts before you even register there's a lion. This is a good thing! Lots of different systems kick in to help you survive. One of those actions is that your adrenal glands, located above your kidneys, send out the hormone epinephrine, also called adrenaline, into your bloodstream. This allows your heart to pump faster and blood to flow through your body quicker. The result is a burst of energy that allows you to make movements to protect your life.

Your adrenal glands also send out another hormone called cortisol. At healthy levels, cortisol manages your sleep cycle and blood pressure as well as equipping your body to recover from the survival response later. When you escape the lion and you're safe again, cortisol aids your body in returning to a normal heartbeat and blood pressure again.

God designed stress to play a protective role in your life. But why do you feel stress when you aren't in physical danger?

The Four Stress Starters

Since lions aren't chasing you every day, why does your body experience stress when you're on a difficult phone call with your mom or when your boss asks about that work assignment? Here's a surprising fact: your autonomic nervous system doesn't know the difference between an actual threat and a perceived threat. This is important to remember. Whether someone is chasing you in an alley, you open an unexpected bill, you're remembering a past negative event, or you're imagining a future problem, your body will trigger a stress response.

I've identified four perceived threats that can trigger a stress response in the body. I call these perceived threats the four stress starters:

- Uncertain—feeling unstable or insecure about an outcome or the future
- Unexpected—being taken by surprise and unable to process or adjust

- Uncontrollable—the inability to manage or fix the situation
- Uncomfortable—feeling uneasy and bothered by what's happening

These four stress starters are nonphysical threats—like emotional lions—that can activate your body's stress response before you even realize it's happening. If you take each of the stress starters and think about a situation in your life, they can cause your heart to beat faster and your blood pressure to go up.

What you may not realize is that perceived threats can be repeated multiple times a day. Every time you think or feel that whatever you're facing is too much for you to handle and you might lose it or fall apart, your body will push adrenaline and cortisol into your bloodstream in hopes of helping you survive that moment. When our bodies flood with those hormones on a regular basis, this is where chronic stress becomes a physical red flag because of elevated blood pressure, cardiovascular issues, frequent illness, and some autoimmune disorders. Registering continuous perceived threats will eventually create real physical damage to your body. It's like leaving your foot pressed on the gas pedal. Never taking your foot off the accelerator will wear your car down faster. Living in constant stress wears down your body and can burn your body out. This shouldn't be cause for shame or self-criticism, but this can be an aha moment that underscores the importance of being aware of what you're thinking, overthinking, or obsessing about.

One of my struggles in my battle against overwhelm was minimizing these symptoms or not recognizing that they were related to each other. I experienced sinus infections every few months before my overwhelm led to burnout. I blamed those infections on the air-conditioning in the building where I worked. Yet, every time, my body was trying to warn me that I needed to adjust my stress level. I ignored it.

Stress versus Stressors

When we're talking about stress, there's an important distinction to be made between our emotional and physical reaction and what we are reacting to. This was an aha moment for me. There is a difference between stress and stressors.

Stress is our reaction, but stressors are the people, places, or things that we are reacting to. A stressor can be a rebellious child, a difficult marriage conflict, an aggressive coworker, or a paycheck that hasn't arrived.

Not everyone reacts the same way to stressors. For example, you may not care about spiders. But I do. My reaction to a spider depends on how big, hairy, or close it is. If all three converge, I can promise you I am about to get loud and embarrassing. If we're together when this happens, you have permission to pretend that you don't know me. However, when I see a snake, nothing happens. My heart rate doesn't change, and my brain doesn't send any panic messages telling my body to get away. Maybe it should, but it doesn't. You might be thinking that a snake is a reason to scream to the rafters and a spider is cute and cuddly. I think you're wrong, but it just goes to show that we all react differently to different stressors. It's helpful for us not to judge someone else's reaction to a situation or matter that doesn't have the same effect on us.

What's crucial, however, is understanding the differences between your stressors and the stress within you. You own your reaction to stress, but you aren't always responsible for the stressors. The focus must shift toward what you can change, which is your reaction. Born with a stutter, pastor Chuck Swindoll is credited with the well-known saying, "Life is 10% what happens to you and 90% how you react to it."

Your job, your kids, your health problems, your spouse— these are not your stress. The danger in seeing them this way is that you will see the people you love or are connected to as trying to hurt you when it is your response that is doing the harm. You're also in danger of seeing your circumstances as a problem rather than an opportunity for God to show up and do something within you that can bless you.

Take a moment right now to identify three people, places, or things that create a stress response inside of you and describe how you respond to them.

STRESSORS	HOW DO YOU REACT?
1.	
2.	
3.	

When our stress leads us to scream at our kids, slam doors, or be rude to our friends or coworkers, that doesn't improve our relationships with them. This doesn't excuse their bad behavior, nor does it mean that you've got to deny or minimize difficult realities in your life. However, identifying the difference between your stressors and your stress can be a game changer by helping you remember that your reaction is your responsibility. When we don't manage that responsibility well, we can wreck not only our mental and emotional health but also our relationships with others.

Let's pause and make this personal. I know that you're thinking of someone or something right now that feels like stress in your life. Satan wants you to confuse your reaction with your relationship in hopes that you'll destroy the relationship with your reaction. Here's a brief stress clarity exercise to refocus your thinking away from blaming someone or something to owning your stress reaction and the consequences. Choose one of the three stressors that you listed above. Fill in the blanks below with that stressor:

_____ is not the cause of my stress.

Even though I feel stress because of _____, I will not blame my reactions on it/them.

Many years ago, my counselor recommended the book *Learning to Tell Myself the Truth* by William Backus, a believer who combines discipleship and psychology for his counseling patients. Backus proposes that we need "truth therapy," which is examining our internal dialogue according to 2 Corinthians 10:5: "We destroy every proud obstacle that keeps people from knowing God. We capture their rebellious thoughts and teach them to obey Christ."[3]

One of the exercises in that book was to write out all my frustrations. I struggled with unmet needs and overwhelm, and I had to reluctantly admit that I harbored a grocery list of unreasonable expectations. I drove to the park with a blanket and a notebook and listed out about ten pages of frustrations with myself and others. I then had to identify a belief that fueled anything I identified as an unmet need, negative self-talk, and expectations. For example, during a frustrating season when I was working full-time but wanted to find a part-time job, I carried resentment because my belief was that the part-time job would solve my problems and I was being kept from what would help me. The reality was that my overwhelm wasn't related to the number of hours I was working; it was because of difficult parenting situations. Reducing my hours would have created a real financial challenge in that season. Identifying that unrealistic expectation didn't make my life easier, but I could shift my belief from blaming my full-time job to being honest about how hard things were at home. I turned the focus back onto myself.

I could choose to take responsibility and challenge those thoughts so that I could release them. Or I could hold on to those thoughts and let them fuel my emotions.

Here is a simple activity you can choose to do. In a notebook or on a sheet of paper, make three columns on the page. In the first column, write down all your frustrations. In the second column, identify each of those as an unmet need, negative self-talk, or an unmet expectation. In the third column, write the belief you hold that creates that frustration. Look at your recent text messages and emails if you need a reference point.

Are you harboring any of these wrong beliefs?

- I am unlovable so that's why people keep letting me down.
- My needs aren't important.
- I must earn love from others.
- People must not love me if they don't change.
- If I work my tail off for others, then they should do the same for me.

Once you have your entire list, then go down the list and release each item one by one. You can say, "I need to release this expectation and will accept my reality as it is."

Wasn't Becoming a Christian Supposed to Take Away My Stress?

There's a lie that says life is easier once a person becomes a Christian. Whether the roots of that lie are embedded in the lips of those who incorrectly teach Scripture or in our own wrong beliefs about God, the result is a type of spiritual disillusionment that leads some people to wonder if their decision to follow Jesus was a mistake.

This is a big topic with a lot of tentacles, like why bad things happen to good people and why God allows evil. While we can't tackle all those questions here, we can establish a baseline of truth from Jesus that might be helpful or freeing for you today, especially if lately your stress or overwhelm has also sparked some confusion in your faith.

Jesus faced one problem after another while He lived on earth. He encountered people problems and faced demonic opposition. Yet, on the night that He was betrayed, Jesus said this to His disciples:

> I have told you all this so that you may have peace in me. Here on earth you will have many trials and sorrows. But take heart, because I have overcome the world. (John 16:33)

While we tend to focus on problems, Jesus leads with peace. He never wants you to lose sight of His promise that not only will you make it through whatever you're experiencing, but you don't have to stress out all the way through it. Furthermore, when your problems feel personal and it seems like God is picking on you, Jesus reminds us that we all face trials. No one, no matter how amazing their life looks on the outside, escapes the hard, heartbreaking, and horrible.

As the author of one-third of the New Testament, the apostle Paul spent his life dealing with stressful circumstances because he followed Jesus. Check out this sobering summary of Paul's experience after becoming a Christian:

> Five different times the Jewish leaders gave me thirty-nine lashes. Three times I was beaten with rods. Once I was stoned. Three times I was shipwrecked. Once I spent a whole night and a day adrift at sea. I have traveled on many long journeys. I have faced danger from rivers and from robbers. I have faced danger from my own people, the Jews, as well as from the Gentiles. I have faced danger in the cities, in the deserts, and on the seas. And I have faced danger from men who claim to be believers but are not. I have worked hard and long, enduring many sleepless nights. I have been hungry and thirsty and have often gone without food. I have shivered in the cold, without enough clothing to keep me warm. Then, besides all this, I have the daily burden of my concern for all the churches. (2 Cor. 11:24–28)

Here Paul lists all the stressors that he was subjected to. I've been through a lot, but I'm grateful that being lashed, stoned, and shipwrecked are things I haven't had to check off my life bingo card so far.

This dramatic overview of Paul's life demonstrates that he was a man who knew what it was like to face all the stress starters. Paul never minimized his challenging experiences, but he never fixated on them either. There's much that you and I can learn from his perspective, which he not only taught but also lived out:

> Yes, everything else is worthless when compared with the infinite value of knowing Christ Jesus my Lord. For his sake I have discarded everything else, counting it all as garbage, so that I could gain Christ. (Phil. 3:8)

Paul never loses sight of God even though his life appears to be a magnet for stressors. Paul never lets his problems obscure his view of God's power or promises.

Do You Want to Get Well?

A huge fear arises in us when we think about whether we can change and about trying something new while we're already overloaded. We wonder if it will work or how long it will take for real relief.

In John 5, Jesus offered a life-changing invitation to a man who'd been waiting thirty-eight years for healing. We don't know why Jesus chose this man. Perhaps Jesus knew that he'd been waiting so long, or maybe because Jesus knew how many of us would share this man's attitude after hearing Jesus's invitation.

Jesus asked the man a simple question: "Would you like to get well?" (v. 6).

Seems like "yes" should be the only answer. Not quite. Here's how the man replied:

> "I can't, sir," the sick man said, "for I have no one to put me into the pool when the water bubbles up. Someone else always gets there ahead of me." (v. 7)

I wonder if the daily defeat of watching people find healing while he couldn't figure out how to make it into the water took away this man's hope. When Jesus offered healing, the man only saw obstacles, not the opportunity for a miracle.

Yet with God, all things are possible.

If you keep reading the story, you'll see that the man is not healed by being put into the water. His healing comes from the power of Jesus's words, which transform and heal the man inside and out.

> Jesus told him, "Stand up, pick up your mat, and walk!" (v. 8)

There's so much in Jesus's encounter with this man to encourage us, especially if we worry that winning the battle of overwhelm is unlikely. Here are two takeaways:

1. *God's path of healing for you is paved with grace, which is His favor that you can't earn.* There's so much grace in this story because the man didn't do anything to earn or deserve healing. In fact, he was surrounded by many others who were suffering and there's no explanation as to why Jesus chose him. We don't even know if this man was a disciple of Christ before or after the miracle. Jesus healed him because Jesus is in the healing business. He simply asked, "Do you want to get well?"

2. *God has promised to break any stronghold in your life, including your stronghold of chronic stress.* Learn from this man and stop letting questions about how you're going to be healed keep you from accepting Jesus's invitation to heal you. He doesn't care if your stress is caused by your past, your self-inflicted pain, guilt, or shame. You may disqualify yourself from the right to be healed, but Jesus hasn't disqualified you.

The beautiful truth about your healing is that it is already waiting for you because it has already been won. Jesus already accomplished this victory for you. If God has the power to raise Jesus from the dead, then God has the power to free you from living chronically stressed. It's waiting if you are willing. Winning the battle of overwhelm looks like living with a calm heart and a peaceful mind. As a result, you live from the power of God's peace so that you can participate in God's eternal purpose.

Now, if you're ready to roll up your sleeves and get to work, let's make sure that you're straight on what you need to do—but more importantly, that you're clear on what God has and has not called you to do.

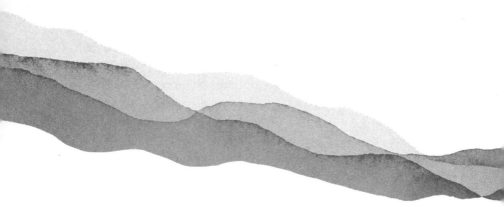

3

GET OFF THE CROSS, HONEY, SOMEBODY NEEDS THE WOOD

It is not the strength of your faith but the object of your faith that actually saves you.

Tim Keller

There's a type of overwhelm that arises from our Christian life that has nothing to do with Jesus but rather religion. It's possible to experience overwhelm when we convince ourselves that we've messed up so much or fallen short so often that we question God's love for us. For example, you might have become distracted by life or simply drifted away from your church and faith just because. The guilt crashes down and you think, "God's probably really mad at me, and I don't know what to do." We assume we've passed the point of no return.

Another type of overwhelm comes from confusion and fear about what we believe, what we should believe, and how to live it out. So many Christians today have so many opinions, and tempers are on a hair trigger. It's overwhelming trying to figure out what God wants us to do when it seems like Christians are fighting among themselves. These days, we're known more for what we're against than what we're for—and we're against a lot. That's overwhelming.

Wondering if God loves you is, in my opinion, the most overwhelming existential question a human, especially a Christian, can ask. If that's you today, I want to share with you the same thing that I believe God's Holy Spirit prompted me to share with an embarrassed young Christian woman who'd been in recovery for opioid abuse and feared God was angry with her: *You can't mess up God's love for you.*

If you need to read that again before you continue, go ahead. You can't mess up God's love for you. There is no condemnation on you. God is still working in you, and when you trust Him, His best is yet to come (Phil. 1:6).

Flowing in the Unforced Rhythms of Grace

Religious stress and overwhelm has a room of spinning plates all its own. Whew. Bless it. You've got a plate spinning for reading your Bible, another for prayer, one hand-me-down plate for still attending your parents' church, a chipped giving plate, a few plates (or a lot of plates!) for volunteering. There's also your small group Bible study plate, even though that tends to go missing—but no worries, you find it every few months and show up again. While all of these are important parts of living the Christian life, the problem arises when you believe that keeping all these plates spinning is what God wants for you. It's not.

Religious stress doesn't come from God but rather from our expectations of what we think God wants from us. We must not confuse religious stress for Holy Spirit conviction. Religious stress is a mindset that believes following rules is essential to following God. There's no peace in our Christian life when we're wrapped up in religious stress.

If there were a picture of religious stress in the dictionary, my face would be there. From the time I accepted Jesus as an eight-year-old kid until my midthirties, I fretted about whether I was doing enough for God. This performance pressure never produced satisfaction in Christ. Only stress.

Religious stress or overwhelm comes from the belief that God wants more *from* us than *for* us. That belief drives the behavior that we must always look for ways to do more for God, and when we fail to do more, then we'd better get busy making up for it. Not only that, but we look at the Christians around us and apply our expectations of what their faith should look like, then either judge them for not being good Christians or envy them for doing the Christian life better than we are.

Jesus didn't live His life on earth in overwhelm or stress. In fact, He spoke against those who piled to-dos on God's people with no regard for how those extra requirements weighed down their hearts. The religious leaders in Jesus's time created religious stress. Jesus offered a different way:

> Come to me, all of you who are weary and carry heavy burdens, and I will give you rest. (Matt. 11:28)

God didn't send Jesus to die to give you more things to do after getting saved. The religious stress that you feel isn't from God. In His great love for us, God sent Jesus to do what we could not do for ourselves—save us. Not only did God save us from the stress of earning forgiveness or salvation through following rules, but He wants us to experience the freedom that comes from our relationship with Him. In *The Message*, Eugene Peterson paraphrases Jesus's invitation this way:

Are you tired? Worn out? Burned out on religion? Come to me. Get away with me and you'll recover your life. I'll show you how to take a real rest. Walk with me and work with me—watch how I do it. Learn the unforced rhythms of grace. I won't lay anything heavy or ill-fitting on you. Keep company with me and you'll learn to live freely and lightly. (Matt. 11:28–30 MSG)

Jesus's invitation offers a chance for you and me to take holy rest from the religious hustle. Can I get an amen? Depending on the denomination or faith tradition you were raised in, you may have been taught that God has a list of requirements— from the number of times per day that you needed to pray, the amount of money that you were required to give, or under what conditions you could be kicked out or shunned from your faith community. All of that is stressful! But Jesus came so that we could lay all of that down and learn His unforced rhythms of grace so that we can live freely and lightly.

Paul is the best example of someone in the Bible who moved from enforcing rules and applying religious stress to others to living by Jesus's unforced rhythms of grace. Before he became the greatest missionary our world has ever known, Paul developed a reputation for his specific skill set: hunting down Christians.

Known at the time as Saul, his Jewish name, Paul was a zealot, someone seriously committed to dotting every *i* and crossing every *t* of the Jewish faith. In Paul's own words, he was as religious as religious could be, from his identification as a Jew to how hard he worked to do all the right things for God:

I am a pure-blooded citizen of Israel and a member of the tribe of Benjamin—a real Hebrew if there ever was one! I was a member of the Pharisees, who demand the strictest obedience to the Jewish law. I was so zealous that I harshly persecuted the church. And as for righteousness, I obeyed the law without fault. (Phil. 3:5–6)

By Saul's time there were 613 laws or rules in the Torah, and Saul aimed to follow each one. As a Pharisee, he believed that it was his duty to make sure that other Jews did the same. So as word spread about Jesus and the gospel of grace declared that Jesus satisfied the requirements of the law, Saul's zeal fired up.

The first mention of Saul in the New Testament comes in Acts 7 at the stoning death of a Jewish follower of Jesus named Stephen, one of seven early church leaders chosen by the twelve apostles after the day of Pentecost. Saul's presence at Stephen's execution is a little footnote in Acts 7:58, which records that those who came to witness Stephen's death laid their coats at Saul's feet. But he wasn't simply a bystander, there to hold the coats of the participants. Saul belonged to the religious sect of the Pharisees, and he sanctioned the death of a fellow Jew. As the people dropped their coats to pick up their stones, Saul watched the scene with an approving eye.

At one point, the Pharisees sent Saul out from Jerusalem to hunt down believers in Damascus. Even though Saul was a significant source of stress for Jewish believers, he didn't see it that way. He truly believed that he was living out God's laws and that throwing people in prison for following Jesus was right and just.

It wasn't until his encounter with the resurrected Jesus on the way to Damascus that Saul realized his zeal for the laws and rules of God wasn't the same as living with zeal for the heart of God. Even as Saul was on his way to imprison believers, Jesus brought the Good News directly to Saul. The gospel should stop us in our tracks and change our direction.

Saul experienced the great exchange from living by religious rules to experiencing a relationship with God through Jesus Christ.

After his encounter with Jesus, Saul was blinded for several days. I wonder if God wanted to make sure that Saul didn't brush aside the encounter and continue going his own way.

Grace should change us. Yet many of us tack grace on to our Christian life instead of letting it lead our life. Grace is the remedy for our religious stress, but only if we let it be.

After encountering Jesus, Saul spent three years in Arabia (Gal. 1:17–18). Not much is known about what Saul did during that time, but he was in the territory around Mount Sinai, the place where Moses met with God to receive the Torah and the site of other spiritually significant Old Testament moments. Author N. T. Wright notes that "Sinai, the great mountain in Arabia, was, in that sense, the place of beginnings."[1]

After his time in Arabia, Saul met with Peter and James before heading back to his hometown of Tarsus for the next fourteen years. There are questions about what Saul did during those years, but I wonder if he spent that time getting to know God relationally instead of through rules. As a religious scholar, Saul would have come to see the Torah in the light of Christ rather than through the rules of legalism. Perhaps Saul needed to spend a chunk of time seeing Jesus as the fulfillment of the Scriptures the way he had spent his youth studying under Jewish rabbis.

In Acts 11, a believer named Barnabas was sent by the church leaders to find Saul in Tarsus. Together, they came back to Antioch and Saul began preaching the gospel. After that, Saul became known by his Greek name, Paul, and he went out as a missionary to share the gospel of grace throughout the world.

Whenever he'd preach in an area, Paul would organize the believers into a church and then stay in touch by writing to them. After Paul left one of those churches he planted in Galatia, a group of Jewish believers began preaching that salvation by grace wasn't enough for a person to be fully and finally saved. They advocated for extra to-dos that the gospel never points to, causing confusion and likely a bunch of stress. Concerned and angered, Paul wrote to that church:

> I am shocked that you are turning away so soon from God, who called you to himself through the loving mercy of Christ. You are following a different way that pretends to be the Good News but is not the Good News at all. You are being fooled by those who deliberately twist the truth concerning Christ. (Gal. 1:6–7)

Paul had learned firsthand that the Good News meant that not only was he forgiven for all that happened in his life before—murder, persecution, and pride—he also didn't have to earn God's favor any longer through following rules. He happily proclaimed himself a slave of Jesus, which would have been freeing considering how as a Pharisee he'd been bound with the chains of religious rules.

Paul called out the Galatian church's legalistic teaching as twisted. Not only that but Paul called down a curse on those who teach a twisted gospel. Paul challenged the believers in Galatia to not get trapped in the rule-following mentality and to remember the freedom Jesus died to bring them. Later in his letter to them he writes:

> I do not treat the grace of God as meaningless. For if keeping the law could make us right with God, then there was no need for Christ to die. (2:21)

We need that reminder as well. Perhaps today you need to include time to reflect on and reconsider the rules that you've followed as a Christian. In the next section of this chapter, we'll talk about a common trap, a disorder that Christian women develop that adds to the stress in their lives.

Later, I'll introduce you to a group of spiritual practices that create space for you to connect with God. These practices aren't rules, nor are they shortcuts or guarantees to automatically eliminating the stress or overwhelm in your life. The spiritual practices aren't to be used as bargaining chips or brownie points to stack up with God. The spiritual practices are intended to create space for you and God, not stress in your relationship with God.

God Didn't Call You to Be Everything to Everybody

There's a solid argument to be made that a good chunk of our overwhelm is the result of our decision to take care of everyone else before taking care of ourselves.

In the movie *Straight Talk*, Dolly Parton's character, Doctor Shirlee, who isn't actually a doctor, becomes a radio sensation as she dispenses homespun wisdom to desperate people. One woman calls into Shirlee's radio show complaining about everything that she did for her loved ones and how tired she was. In response to the woman's ruffled feathers, Doctor Shirlee offers this advice: "Get off the cross, honey. Somebody needs the wood."[2]

If you can hear those words in Dolly Parton's voice, that line sounds even better. The point here is that there is only one Savior of your friends, your family, and your life, and it's Jesus, not you.

No one has asked us to set ourselves on fire to keep other people warm, but far too many of us do. There have been many times in my life when I've been stressed because I took on way too much. Instead of saying no or asking for help, I'd walk around the house or office giving off the periodic deep sigh of an overworked victim of her own making. Is this just me or can you relate? Switching back to the illustration of spinning plates, how many of your plates spin because you want to earn love or approval from others, you're prone to perfectionism, or you struggle with letting go of control?

God has not asked or commanded you to be everything to everybody. Jesus's invitation to experience His unforced rhythms of grace isn't just for you to experience for yourself. It's for you to apply to your relationships with others. God didn't create you to wear yourself out or stress yourself out over someone else's relationship with God or how they are living their life.

I remember a saying that was popular in youth groups: JOY stands for Jesus first, others next, and you last. This pithy little ditty attempts to mirror Jesus's teaching in Matthew 22:37–39:

> "You must love the LORD your God with all your heart, all your soul, and all your mind." This is the first and greatest commandment. A second is equally important: "Love your neighbor as yourself."

Jesus taught that we're to love others with the same love that we apply to ourselves. Unfortunately, some interpret these verses to mean that we need to give everything we have to God and others while minimizing the value of loving ourselves. This error in interpretation rewires the DNA of our beliefs into thinking that if we love someone then it's okay to drain ourselves of health, hope, and good common sense to help them.

In their bestselling book *Burnout*, authors Emily and Amelia Nagoski introduce a complex condition called the Human Giver Syndrome, which they characterize as a virus that infects a human being, driving him or her to believe that being of service to others is the highest value in life, even if those endless acts of service destroy the giver in the process. The authors leverage research and professional experience on how to handle cycles of stress, but they admit that they were unable to speak to the spiritual aspects of overwhelm or burnout.[3]

I coined the term Good Christian Woman Disorder as the Jesus-loving, saved cousin to the Human Giver Syndrome. The Good Christian Woman Disorder begins with a woman who says yes to faith in Christ, but without healthy support, helpful boundaries, or God-honoring guidance, mutations can occur like cancer cells. The Good Christian Woman Disorder is curable, but if it is not cured, it will be costly.

While "good" may sound like an admirable thing, it is all about self-effort and obligation instead of grace. Good Christian Woman Disorder takes our expectations plus our wrong interpretations of Scripture plus our personal life experiences plus the struggle with sin, and the sum total is a guilt-inducing, legalistic, overwhelming experience with faith that God never intended.

Do you struggle with Good Christian Woman Disorder? Here are some identifiers that capture the disorder's attitudes, beliefs, and behaviors. Put a check mark beside any that resonate with you:

_____ You think that there is an ideal Christian life and that if you aren't experiencing it, then you are doing something wrong.

_____ Your goal as a Christian woman is to serve everyone you can in Jesus's name, even though it takes away time for your own self-care.

_____ You do everything in your power to always make Jesus and your family look good.

_____ You think saying no or enforcing healthy personal boundaries is disrespectful to others, especially if those "others" are your pastor or church leaders.

_____ You don't allow yourself to cry, be depressed, or struggle with sin because to do those things is a sign that you don't have a strong faith.

As we carry those wrong beliefs about God and what it means to be a follower of Christ, we feel increased pressure to be perfect, to do more to look like a good Christian. At the same time, we hide anything that makes us look less than perfect, whether it's sin, a struggle, a fear, or even our questions about God. The gap between our good Christian mask and our authentic self widens, and stress fills that space until the dissonance eventually becomes so painful that it overwhelms us. We lose sight of what it even means to be a Christian because while we tried to live for Jesus, we didn't understand grace and it was too hard.

If you struggle or suffer from Good Christian Woman Disorder, here are some important reminders for you:

1. You can't mess up God's unconditional love for you (Jer. 31:3; Rom. 8:39).
2. God wants more *for* you than *from* you (Jer. 29:11; Phil. 1:6).
3. God wants you to receive His transforming power, not live by your self-righteousness (Gal. 5:22–25).
4. Grace is a gift to bring you peace (Eph. 2:8).

If this is an area of overwhelm in your life, I encourage you to look up the verses referenced above. Since God's Word is living and active, you need the truth of His Word to cut through and remove the "Good Christian" wrong beliefs that rob you of God's peace.

I also encourage you to pray. In fact, if you need words, you can use these:

God, thank You for Your faithfulness and love for me. I believe that You want more for me than from me. Help me to let go of the belief that I need to earn Your love or my salvation. I want to embrace the unforced rhythms of grace made possible in Christ. Amen.

4

SEEING GOD'S BIG PICTURE BEYOND STRESS

God designed the human machine to run on Himself.

C. S. Lewis

As Paul wrote letters to churches all over the first-century world, he faced constant stressors and he humbly admitted to experiencing overwhelm. There's no direct reference to a specific incident, but whatever Paul went through was a lot to handle:

> We think you ought to know, dear brothers and sisters, about the trouble we went through in the province of Asia. We were crushed and overwhelmed beyond our ability to endure, and we thought we would never live through it. In fact, we expected to die. But as a result, we stopped relying on ourselves and learned to rely only on God, who raises the dead. And he did rescue us from mortal danger, and he will rescue us again. We have

placed our confidence in him, and he will continue to rescue us. (2 Cor. 1:8–10)

Paul's audience in Corinth was likely shocked by his admission of feeling overwhelmed. At that time, Stoicism was popular in Corinth. Stoics believed that when going through hard times, the goal was to eliminate all human reaction or response. One Stoic philosopher told her students, "Men, if you heed me, wherever you may be, whatever you may be doing, you will feel no pain, no anger, no compulsion, no hindrance, but you will pass your lives in tranquility and in freedom from every disturbance."[1]

At face value, arriving at the point where nothing ever bothers you seems attractive. The mechanic calls to tell you that your engine block is cracked. *No feelings about that.* The IRS sends a letter stating that you owe thousands in back taxes. *No feelings about that.* Your loving mother battles cancer for five years before dying a difficult death. *No feelings*—wait, what? Shouldn't you feel some emotion?

Denying what should naturally be happening inside of us isn't the same as peace. God didn't create you with emotions only for you to ignore them. Diminishing our natural human emotions or stress reactions can shut down our empathy for others and our opportunity to experience joy. Even more dangerous, as author Chip Dodd warns, "Wherever you lack awareness in your heart, no room exists for God."[2] As attractive as numbing out might seem when you're feeling stressed-out or burned-out, that's not actually peace. In fact, the fullest, most delicious gift of peace is that your calmness comes from your abiding in the presence and power of God. This is why peace is stronger than your stress. Peace allows you to face any hardship in life and still experience joy, grace, purpose, and more. You can't experience those gifts of life if you've shut down or numbed out.

We're only human. Paul describes us as jars of clay, full of capacity yet fragile and guaranteed to be broken at some point in our lives (2 Cor. 4:7). Without God's strength, we remain broken, scraping through life, hoping that our chipped edges and stress cracks can withstand the pressure that never seems to let up. On the flip side, Paul points out that when the life of Jesus flourishes within us, there's a supernatural glow-up that does more than just shine brightly; there's a strength in that shine that points to the power and glory of God. It's the shine that causes people to say, "Wow, you've been through a lot, yet you look like you're doing okay." Then we can respond and say, "Yes, I don't look like what I've been through, because God's strength is bringing me through it."

Here's how Paul describes our stronger-than-stress victory:

> We are pressed on every side by troubles, but we are not crushed. We are perplexed, but not driven to despair. We are hunted down, but never abandoned by God. We get knocked down, but we are not destroyed. Through suffering, our bodies continue to share in the death of Jesus so that the life of Jesus may also be seen in our bodies. (2 Cor. 4:8–10)

Whenever I read these verses, it's easy for my eyes to gravitate toward the first phrase in each verse describing the hardship. Yet, the hope is found in the second phrase of each verse. For every hardship, heartache, or horror that you may face in life, Paul says that in Christ:

You are not crushed.

You are not driven to despair.

You are not abandoned.

You are not destroyed.

Whether you're in a season of stress or your middle name is overwhelm, my deepest desire is for you to find yourself in the sweet, juicy middle of God's presence, power, and promises.

The next and most important step in your journey is recognizing a perspective shift that you need to make when looking at yourself, your problems, and the future. After we explore that, I'll teach you how to apply that perspective shift and find relief in what I like to call "the Breathing Room."

Choosing God's Big Picture Instead of Our Small Screen

It's no secret that we're looking down on the world more than before. I'm talking not just figuratively but literally. Our cell phones have drawn our heads down to focus on the screens in front of us. With few exceptions, we've become accustomed to handling our entire world on our devices. With just a few keystrokes, we can pay bills, let our kids know we're running late, or impulsively order another pair of shoes. Oh wait . . . maybe that last one is just me.

Thanks to technology, we're led to believe that what we can see on our phones is not only a reflection of the power that we have but the perspective that shapes our daily movements in our individual worlds. At this time in history, there are lots of conversations about online platforms and how the content that we choose informs the kinds of content that those platforms will suggest. So, even though we think that our phones empower us to better handle the world around us, they simply feed us more of the world that we've created for ourselves.

I don't want to attach too many value statements to smartphones. I'd rather focus on this question: How much of our stress response is because of shrinking our view of God and trying to fit Him into our small-screen perspective? If God is only as big as what you can find out on Google, then your quest to overcome your stress will feel hopeless.

There's another perspective. It's what I call *God's Big Picture*.

God's Big Picture encompasses the entire universe from the beginning to the end of time. Compare that to our cell phone screens and you'll recognize our limited and flawed perspective. Here's a visualization of God's Big Picture versus our small screen:

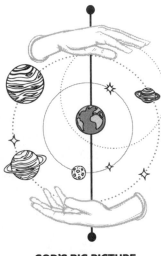 

GOD'S BIG PICTURE   **OUR SMALL SCREEN**

I don't have to list the scientific measurements of the universe versus your smartphone to offer a spiritual illustration of the difference between how God sees everything and the limitations of what you can see. But considering these two perspectives, certain realities stand out:

God's Big Picture	Our Small Screen
Knowledge of all things always, from eternity past to eternity future.	Incomplete knowledge of ourselves and the world around us.
Weaves together all things with supernatural sovereignty and power regardless of time or distance.	Connection is limited to our capacity and our limited lifetime.
Governed by His holiness and divine unconditional love for each person.	Driven by our self-interest and undermined by our fears.
Cannot be sabotaged or stopped by anyone or anything.	Subject to interference by oppositional spiritual forces and our own sin.

We're going to leave Paul's story for a moment and travel further back in Scripture to an Old Testament passage that provides a helpful snapshot into God's Big Picture versus our small-screen perspective. In Deuteronomy 30:4–6, Moses gives a prophetic word foretelling a difficult season for the Israelites in future generations:

> Even though you are banished to the ends of the earth, the LORD your God will gather you from there and bring you back again. The LORD your God will return you to the land that belonged to your ancestors, and you will possess that land again. Then he will make you even more prosperous and numerous than your ancestors!
>
> The LORD your God will change your heart and the hearts of all your descendants, so that you will love him with all your heart and soul and so you may live!

At that time, God's people were just about to enter the promised land. If you were an Israelite living in that season, you'd be really excited about getting out of the desert and settled into a new home and not really concerned about what would befall unfortunate people years later. What the people listening that day couldn't know was that the time between Moses's prophecy and God's ultimate fulfillment of it would be hundreds of years.

Those three verses would encompass dozens of kings, countless battles and supernatural circumstances, and millions of ways that God showed up in the lives of His people. Centuries later, around 586 BC, as most scholars agree, the prophetic word came to pass. The Israelites were embarking on a new normal that looked a lot like an ongoing, overwhelming nightmare.

After King Nebuchadnezzar's vast Assyrian army surrounded the walls of Jerusalem, invaded the city, and carried off a large segment of the population, no doubt the stress levels of the Israelites shot through the roof, and for good reason.

As generations of family members were separated from each other, no doubt innocent people were accidently or intentionally killed in the process. Then there were those who watched as long lines of their fellow Jews were marched away, not knowing which was worse—being left behind or on that road to captivity. Can you imagine the shock of seeing your life left behind as you were marched off into the unknown?

However, something curious happens. It's in this season that a prophet named Jeremiah receives some unique and interesting words from God, giving the Jewish people instructions on how to live in their stressful situation. These instructions don't seem to make sense considering the level of daily stress they must have been experiencing. Pay attention to what God tells them to do and how He tells them to live:

> This is what the Lord of Heaven's Armies, the God of Israel, says to all the captives he has exiled to Babylon from Jerusalem: "Build homes, and plan to stay. Plant gardens and eat the food they produce. Marry and have children. Then find spouses for them so that you may have many grandchildren. Multiply! Do not dwindle away! And work for the peace and prosperity of the city where I sent you into exile. Pray to the Lord for it, for its welfare will determine your welfare." (Jer. 29:4–7)

If you're not handling your overwhelm well, the last thing you want is some guy to show up and say, "So, God wanted me to tell you that even though it's really bad now, go ahead and live like everything is normal."

God knew the big picture of the Israelites' story, so He wasn't surprised that they became unwilling residents of Babylon. He instructed them to rebuild their lives and look toward the future, even though there were times when they were overwhelmed.

It took a few years for me to stop obsessing about the reasons why I was stressed. I fully believed that if I could fix those reasons, then I'd be at peace. There was a codependence that I hated, but it was my reality. My happiness was held hostage by the circumstances in my life. But God wanted more for me. He wanted to give me hope.

I began to shift from my small-screen Barb perspective to God's Big Picture and to filter my life through it. Gaining that eternal perspective transformed how I woke up in the morning. Rather than seeing each day as a capsule of isolated events that I needed to figure out, I learned to enlarge my view of God by shifting the focus to Him and getting curious about what He was doing in me and around me. I started asking questions like:

In this tough moment, what do I need to remember about God?

As I reflect on today, how did I see God taking care of me and my family?

How can I pray for others who are going through what I'm going through?

As my commitment to my place in God's Big Picture grew, I felt less overwhelmed because my view of God was bigger and my problems took on a new perspective in light of eternity. Like Paul, I realized that I wasn't crushed; I was hopeful and not in despair because I knew that God was giving me a power each day that made me stronger than my stress.

Perhaps it might be helpful for you to pause here to answer those three questions above and reflect on them for your own life.

Just a few verses later, Jeremiah delivers words that are familiar to many of us, but I want you to look at them with fresh eyes.

"For I know the plans I have for you," says the LORD. "They are plans for good and not for disaster, to give you a future and a hope." (v. 11)

God knows everything that you don't know. The important question for you is whether you know what is true about God. Just because you believe that God knows everything, it doesn't mean that you trust Him with everything in your life. God invites you to live for more than just this life; He invites you to do life with Him so that He can leave a legacy of faith through you.

The last word of Jeremiah 29:11 is my favorite: *hope*. Hope is knowing that there is good to come. In God's Big Picture, hope is the frame. The Hebrew word translated as "hope" is *tiqvah*, which can also mean "cord" or "rope."[3] This references the story of Rahab in Joshua 2–6, and how she left a scarlet rope outside her window so that when the Israelites invaded Jericho, she and her family would be saved. She hung that rope not knowing how or when God would save her, yet Rahab trusted that He would. Hope holds on to that same trust in God. We may not know how God will show up, but we believe that He will.

While we're waiting on God, that doesn't mean we're helpless in our room full of spinning plates. It's important for us to learn how to create some breathing room for ourselves to prepare for God to work.

Stop by the Breathing Room

Every Thanksgiving, there's an important question that I ask myself (and my pants) between my second and third plates of food: "If you eat this, will you still have breathing room?" You know what I'm talking about, right? It's the room that you need to catch your breath so that you can be comfortable.

Apart from the holidays, "breathing room" is the phrase that I use whenever I need to pause or create space to refocus or resettle myself. For example, I like to add at least thirty minutes of breathing room or margin between Zoom calls. I need an hour of breathing room to calm myself down after a heated discussion.

Do you know how much breathing room you need and when? It's a good question to think about. Breathing room also serves a more immediate purpose of providing emergency relief during spikes of stress in your life.

The Breathing Room is the name that I've created to describe the necessary space that helps you create a pause. We need pauses to prevent the onset of stress and overwhelm or to back ourselves down from a stress spike or wave of overwhelm before we shift into survival mode physical responses. Human beings are an integration of mind, body, and spirit. All three elements are intertwined with each other. In the previous chapter, we learned how the mind can trigger the body to react to a perceived threat. The good news is that when you learn how to use the Breathing Room, you can also teach your body how to *not* react to a perceived threat or how to deactivate any survival mode physical reaction. In addition to helping your body not react to the perceived threat, the Breathing Room creates space for you to emotionally regulate. As you master these breathing exercises, you'll give yourself a chance to refocus your thoughts, which can redirect your emotions. That is emotional regulation, and it reflects Paul's instruction in Romans 12:2, which teaches us to make room and allow the Holy Spirit to change the way we think.

There are two Breathing Room exercises that I want to share with you.

Breathing Room Exercise #1

As a life coach, one of the first activities I walk clients through is a breathing exercise. Often clients arrive from work, from running errands, or amid a stress reaction, so they aren't ready to settle into their coaching work. They need a pause to prepare. There are lots of breathing exercises, but the one I use is a stripped-down version of the CALM technique I introduced in my book *Winning the Worry Battle*. This exercise coaches the mind, body, and spirit back to calm by displacing the mental thoughts that are reacting to the four stress starters (uncertain, unexpected, uncontrollable, uncomfortable) and also slowing down the heart rate so that the body stops reacting to the perceived threat and triggering the fight, flight, or freeze survival response.

1. Take a slow inhale breath, counting to five.
2. Hold the breath for the count of five.
3. Release your breath while saying the word "Mississippi."
4. Repeat steps 1–3 five times.

This exercise slows down your heart rate, which communicates safety to your body and deactivates the survival response, and the word "Mississippi" is complicated enough to disrupt the racing, worried, or catastrophic thoughts in your mind. I suggest using this tool anytime you start to feel anxiety or overwhelm in your gut or your thoughts start racing. Giving yourself that breathing room will save you time, prevent emotional outbursts, and enable you to invite God into your situation much sooner.

Breathing Room Exercise #2: SOS Soul Soothing

As humans, we need to know three things: that we are safe, that we are loved, and that our needs are met. SOS soul soothing uses important reminders of God's constant care. SOS stands for *stressed, overwhelmed, struggling,* so these are three cues for when you can use this tool.

I developed this exercise for myself as a reminder of God's security and safety for me when perceived threats—for example, relationship problems, frustrations at work, or fears for the future—threaten to push me into overwhelm.

Repeat the following statements to yourself:

1. I am safe and not in physical danger.
2. I am secure and I trust God to provide everything that I need.
3. I am unconditionally loved by God and He is with me right now.

Would you consider using one or both Breathing Room exercises today, just to try them out? It's important that you develop a habit of creating breathing room for yourself not only to coach your body out of stress reactions but also to set yourself up for success when you learn the spiritual practices. Even if you question whether there will ever be an ideal time for you to pause and spend time with God, these exercises can prepare your heart, spirit, and body as well as help you calm down whenever life's problems distract you while you're spending time with God.

If you want to get extra fancy during your Breathing Room exercises, light a candle to create a focal point, regardless of whether your eyes are open or closed. Lighting a candle is a symbol of God's presence that can remind us of how God led the Israelites by a pillar of fire at night (Exod. 13:21–22) and how the presence of the Holy Spirit appeared as flames of fire on the day of Pentecost (Acts 2:3).

When you remember God's Big Picture amid your everyday life, you can hold on to hope that God's story for you isn't limited to one stressful day after another. He wants His glory to shine through your story. I love Paul's words in 2 Corinthians 1:10, where he writes, "We have placed our confidence in him, and he will continue to rescue us."

That's the confidence that God wants you to have in Him.

5

STRONGER THAN STRESS

It's not the load that breaks you down, it's the way you
carry it.

Lou Holtz

Jesus was no stranger to stress and overwhelm. There is a
powerful scene in Matthew 26 where we see Jesus in the garden of Gethsemane grappling with everything that was about to
happen to Him on Calvary's cross. Luke's abbreviated account
of that story includes this important detail:

He [Jesus] prayed more fervently, and he was in such agony
of spirit that his sweat fell to the ground like great drops of
blood. (Luke 22:44)

This detail conveys an intensity of stress that few can com-
prehend. Sweating drops of blood is a very rare condition called
hematohidrosis. Under extreme stress, the tiny blood vessels

around our sweat glands can rupture and release blood through our skin. While Jesus is God incarnate, He also encountered every aspect of our human experience, including extreme stress. This is so meaningful for me because in the moments when I question whether anyone can understand what I am going through, I am always reminded that Jesus understands.

In that Gethsemane moment, however, I am grateful that Jesus knew the difference between the intense stress that He experienced and the stressors, namely humanity, that He chose to die for. If Jesus had not been God and had only been human, like me, He could have looked at our sinful human state and how He'd been treated while on earth and said, "These people are stressing me out. They are not going to appreciate everything that I'm about to go through for them. Forget this!"

Aren't you so glad that Jesus was committed to God's Big Picture spiritual vision for humanity? He knows that we can't get ourselves together on any level on our own. We can't. Or as my Tennessee-born, redheaded grandfather used to say, *we cain't.* We—both you and me—need a Savior. Notice how I didn't say that we needed a Savior in the past tense, but each day we need Jesus and the ongoing saving work of the gospel of grace in our lives. We need a Savior for our eternal security, we need a Savior to rescue our mental health, and we need a Savior as an anchor amid the ebb and flow of our emotional wellness.

As Jesus fell to His knees on the ground with speckles of watery, bloody sweat covering Him and an emotional tornado swirling within Him, He never lost sight of His love for us. He knew that the gift of grace that we need to unlock eternity with God wouldn't come unless He hung on that cross and died. At the same time, God knew that Jesus's body needed strength. Luke captures that moment too:

Then an angel appeared from heaven and strengthened him. (22:43)

God gave Jesus additional strength when He needed it. So, if Jesus needed additional strength and God sent it, how much more will God do that for you?

The Difference between Strength and Survival Mode

As a Black woman, I've seen a pervasive stereotype in my culture known as the "strong Black woman." This phrase describes a Black woman who has endured under overwhelming circumstances in response to cultural pressures that are specific to Black women. While it's meant to be a compliment, Black women who wear this label aren't celebrating. Generations of Black women have survived the consequences of families being torn apart during slavery and often raising children alone due to the well-documented disparities in healthcare, pay inequality, and the disproportionate number of Black males who are incarcerated. Instead of an uproar that a Black woman is forced to survive in these conditions, she's given the label "strong Black woman." But is that strength?

In June 2023, the Exhale app, the first emotional well-being app for Black women, published a report titled "The State of Self-Care for Black Women" in which over one thousand Black women were surveyed. Of those respondents, 25 percent reported being hospitalized or needing medical care due to stress. "An overwhelming 76% believe that there is a prevalence of people who believe Black women are stronger than most people and should be able to manage more stress than others."[1] My takeaway from this is the cultural acceptance of normalizing a Black woman's life in survival mode.

Including this particular conversation doesn't minimize what other women from other races and ethnicities must do to survive. I write about the strong Black woman stereotype because that is what I know. I've been given that label more times than I'd like. Without God, I would be a Black woman living in survival mode.

There's a famous quote that says "what doesn't kill you makes you stronger." Those words linger on the lips of a woman crawling through chaos and overwhelm as she's trying to find hope and meaning for what she's going through. The quote asserts that suffering makes us stronger—again, in an effort to provide meaning for the madness. But strength is not the automatic result of suffering.[2] While not all stress leads to suffering, all suffering is stressful; yet there is the potential for suffering to lead to strength. At the same time, we cannot forget that just because something doesn't kill us and has the potential to make us stronger, there will be a physical, emotional, or relational price tag for that acquired strength.

Survival after suffering and strength after suffering are two different things. *Survival* is continuing to live or exist in spite of an accident, ordeal, or difficult circumstance, whereas *strength* is the capacity to withstand pressure or great force. How many of us confuse survival mode for strength?

Survival mode reminds me of a line from a Mary Oliver poem where she asks, "Are you living just a little and calling it a life?"[3] Every overwhelmed woman longs for a better life than the one where she's crawling through her day, collapsing into bed for a few hours of poor sleep, and doing it all over again the next day. To everyone around you, your survival mode can look productive, impressive, desperate, or anything in between. You can fool a lot of people by tossing up a few cute photos on social media.

Survival mode keeps you spinning along with the plates that you're trying to keep going. Every day you live in the anxious race of rushing from one urgent matter to the next while hoping that the important matters you can't get to can wait. Survival mode looks like consuming caffeine because you can't make enough time for sleep. Survival mode looks like fast food, retail therapy, or impulse buying because you need to make quick, convenient decisions even if they aren't the best ones.

If you want to, you can fancy up your survival mode so that people don't see it on you. Add sunglasses, an Instagram filter, and pictures of you drinking a fancy iced coffee. No one will know that you rage-shopped, clearing out your Amazon cart while crying only minutes before.

One day, I drove to my summer Bible study group wearing the same clothes that I'd slept in the night before. During that season, my kids were having a hard time, my room of spinning plates looked more like an acre of plates, and I was in the midst of a heavy love affair with Snickers bars. Yet I showed up at that Bible study every week and didn't say a word about how I felt like I was underwater and drowning every day. Nope, I skirted the "How are you?" question each week by bringing up something cool or funny that my kids were doing. I couldn't risk talking about me or else I'd cry, and I couldn't let that happen in front of my Christian friends. Christians were always supposed to be happy and full of joy, right?

Halfway to the meeting, I noticed my wrinkled clothes and panicked. I stopped and bought a new outfit so that I could at least look like I had it together even if that was far from the truth.

When life is overwhelming and you're living in survival mode, you adapt to one of the survival responses that your body uses when you're in physical danger. Overwhelm is a mix of emotions, and as Christian psychiatrist and author Curt Thompson points out, "The origin of our word *emotion* is ground in the idea of e-motion, or preparing for motion. . . . We cannot separate what we feel from what we do."[4] When you're in survival mode, you'll react because the emotions triggering your stress will cause a reaction.

In chapter 4, we learned about the autonomic nervous system and how it equips our bodies to respond to threats by triggering one of the following survival stress responses:

Fight: to physically defend yourself against the attack
Flight: to escape from danger
Freeze: to play dead and hope that the threat loses interest

We have those same survival responses when it comes to perceived threats, plus one more. Instead of three responses, there are four responses here because *fawn* has been added in recent years as a stress response. I developed the following chart to show how the four survival responses look and common phrases that you might say when facing a perceived threat.

Survival reaction	What it looks like	Common phrases associated with it
Fight	Immediately activating a plan to combat the problem without considering whether the problem is within one's control or is appropriate for one to solve, and often while lacking the wisdom, planning, or patience to solve the problem effectively.	"I've got to do something to fix this right now!" "Just do something!" "Hurry up and figure something out."
Flight	Avoidance of the problem because it's too overwhelming or confusing. Also, an unwillingness to wait for the problem to be worked out.	"I'll deal with that later." "Let someone else figure that out." "This is stupid. I quit."
Freeze	Denying that the problem exists or refusing to address the blind spots that might be contributing to the problem or its consequences. Can include the silent treatment or ghosting.	"I don't know what to say." "I don't want to talk about it."
Fawn	Appealing to the threat in hopes of appeasing or minimizing the threat. This response also includes ignoring one's own needs in order to appear helpful and friendly. The inability to say no is a common feature in this survival response.	"What do you think I should do?" "Oh, no. Don't worry about me. I don't need that for myself." "Can I wait to see what _____ wants me to do?"

Which survival responses do you gravitate toward more naturally? If I had to pick two, I would pick fight and fight. Yes, I said that twice. When I'm stressed and in survival mode, I'm fighting to figure out how to fix, change, or improve a situation. That may sound admirable, but my motive is reducing my stress, not necessarily seeing what's best for the long-term in that situation.

You might naturally lean toward a different response. We don't need to villainize our survival responses. They are a sign that we are doing the best that we can. It truly is okay to not be okay. The good news is that God has a path away from "not okay" that leads to His peace.

What you need to be aware of are the following behaviors that can cause your survival mode to snowball into overwhelm. You've heard of the four horsemen of the apocalypse? I call these the four horsemen of overwhelm.

Overfunctioning—doing too much

Overthinking—being unable to find clarity or make decisions

Obsessing—fixating on your expectations or a certain outcome

Overloaded—feeling burdened by the past, guilt, or others' expectations

In chapter 16, I'll address how you can apply the spiritual practices to these expressions of overwhelm. Yet, in order for those later tools to be lasting and effective, you first need the bedrock foundation of God's inner peace.

God desires to equip you with an inner strength. Paul writes about this in Ephesians 3:16–17:

I pray that from his glorious, unlimited resources he will empower you with inner *strength* through his Spirit. Then Christ will make his home in your hearts as you trust in him. Your roots will grow down into God's love and keep you *strong*.

God has what you lack and He generously provides everything that you need. There's no reason to live in overwhelm when God has His abundance to give to you. Instead of living each day in survival mode, you can receive inner strength from God directly through His Holy Spirit. God's strength is the fuel for your resilience. Unlike our human strength, which can be depleted, God's strength is an unending supernatural source that steadies you and sets you up for the abundant life of faith, adventure, and purpose that Jesus promised. Survival mode is a life of just getting by, but when you know that you're stronger than your stress, no amount of difficulty can stop you from living out God's eternal plan for your life.

What does inner strength look like? In a word, *peace*. The inner unbotheredness that can only come from a deeper, stronger, unshakable source within. It's hard to picture what that looks like if you've never experienced it, but there's a beautiful visual of it that an artist painted following a devastating event.

After an F5 tornado leveled his hometown of Joplin, Mississippi, artist Jack Dawson painted his famous work *Peace in the Midst of the Storm*, which depicts the side of a mountain with two rivers of wild water rushing over the edge during a storm and a dramatic lightning show in the distance. The background is a mix of black and navy with no sunlight. Tucked into the side of a tiny mountain crevice in the bottom half of the painting is a nest with a sleeping dove. The bird is snuggled down and unbothered by the chaos all around. If the painting were brought to life, we'd see its little birdie chest smoothly rising and falling in an even rhythm.[5]

I love that the dove is asleep instead of sitting up or pacing back and forth at high alert. Settling down to sleep in the middle of chaos isn't easy to do. Biologically, we must feel physically and psychologically safe to fall asleep.[6] How many times have you lain awake or paced because you were unable to settle down and feel secure enough to fall asleep? Peace is the presence of calm even in the middle of chaos.

When Jack Dawson's mother looked at his painting, she remarked about how the bird was at peace even as the darkness, symbolizing evil, was all around. The dove in the painting represents the kind of calm and tranquility that we all want when the kids make bad decisions, you forgot about that 9 a.m. Zoom meeting, or your car insurance rates increase again.

God's promise is for you to experience His peace that expresses itself as strength. That kind of strong peace steadies you in the knowledge of God's secure love and care amid the storms of life. You can sleep unbothered like that bird and be strong enough to face whatever comes in the light of day.

From his prison cell in Rome, Paul wrote to the Philippian church about the protective strength of peace:

> Don't worry about anything; instead, pray about everything. Tell God what you need, and thank him for all he has done. Then you will experience God's peace, which exceeds anything we can understand. His peace will guard your hearts and minds as you live in Christ Jesus. (Phil. 4:6–7)

The peace that Paul writes about here is the same peace that Jesus spoke of to His disciples as the gift for their hearts and minds. This peace is more than calm. It is the fullest expression of what Old Testament authors referred to as *shalom* or a wholeness within oneself. The word used in New Testament Greek is *eiréné*, which also means wholeness and well-being.[7]

Notice that Paul describes how peace protects us when our hearts want to respond to a threat. For peace to be able to do that, there must be a strength to it. What is it shielding your heart from? Anything that you perceive as a threat—whenever you're thinking or doing something and suddenly experience an unsettled moment.

Peace says, "Oh, I see that, but you're okay. No need to let this rile you up. Take a deep breath." When something bad does happen, peace says, "Yes, this is hard. Yes, this breaks your heart, but God won't let it break you." Peace protects you from hopelessness and discouragement and keeps you from living in survival mode.

I love meaningful acronyms, so I looked at Philippians 4:7 and created one to define how God's peace that passes all understanding makes you stronger than your stress.

Patience: calmly waiting on God's timeline

Endurance: remaining faithful in difficult circumstances

Appreciation: maintaining a heart of gratitude toward God

Confidence: believing God's character and promises

Eternal Plan: keeping a long-term perspective in every moment

This is what being stronger than stress looks like. The spiritual practices that you'll learn in the coming chapters will show you some of the ways to create space for God to expand His strengthening peace within you.

If you were to do a side-by-side comparison of peace versus survival mode, it would look like this:

Peace		Survival mode
Patience	instead of	Impulsivity
Endurance	instead of	Exhaustion
Appreciation	instead of	Anger or frustration
Confidence	instead of	Insecurity or fear
Eternal plan	instead of	Urgency of the moment

There's more to life than living stressed, overwhelmed, and in survival mode. It is possible to live beyond the desire to just de-stress and instead experience God's best and highest blessing for us, which is His perfect peace. However, the beauty of God's perfect peace is that He builds it into us. It's not an instant fix that He slaps on top of our circumstances like a Band-Aid. Rather, God's perfect peace soaks into our spiritual DNA and transforms everything about how we react, respond, and receive whatever happens to us in this life. God's perfect peace is deep and wide and lasting, but it is also a process that happens over time.

This is where we experience tension when introducing the idea of spiritual practices. We've got to get honest about the fact that we prefer Band-Aids over deep healing or transformation.

Spiritual practices are tools or methods that help us to connect with God. If you google the term "spiritual practices" (also called disciplines), you'll find a flood of gurus out there who offer different practices to help you calm down, relax, or experience peace. At the end of the rainbow of those spiritual practices, the individual is supposed to be more connected with themselves or with the universe. Various methods include New Age elements like chanting, chakras, or crystals. Perhaps you have even followed some of that spiritual advice. There's a whole conversation that we can have about the dangers of following spiritual practices that do not lead to a Jesus-centered, gospel-focused connection with God. For the most part, New Age spiritual practices apply Band-Aids that poison you with demonic power instead of bringing transformative peace.

To be clear, when I use the term "spiritual practices," I am referring only to methods that center a sovereign, holy, almighty God as part of our Christian faith. Now, let's say that you aim to do this. Why you center God is just as important as how you center Him. Maybe you aren't looking for a spiritual quick fix like the secular gurus teach. But if you're being honest, do you secretly hope that if you get great at executing the spiritual practices then you can prove to God how serious you are, and maybe He'll cash your practice points for His favor?

On their own, godly spiritual practices do not have supernatural transformative power. Spiritual practices are a workout for your spirit—and sometimes they will make you sweat just like at the gym. Spiritual practices focus on training our inner selves. We can't train our inner selves, only God can. Spiritual practices put us in a position to experience the greatness and magnificence of God, something that we need when we're overwhelmed with life. My experience of overwhelm is often because of my scarcity mentality of not enough. My problems always seem bigger than my view of God. For me, spiritual practices have created room for me to enlarge my view of God in different ways. As I experience different expressions of His power, presence, and provision, my peace grows because I know that God is bigger than everything that can overwhelm me.

Of course, every chapter will include specifics and creative ideas on how to apply these spiritual practices in your real-life context so that you can experience God's gift of peace in the places where you are now experiencing stress. Changing your reaction to stress will transform your level of peace as well as improve your relationships and your personal well-being.

It's time to give yourself permission to jump into this journey of exploring and learning about the ten spiritual practices. Even if you're already familiar with the overall concepts, I believe that there are fresh insights and spiritual wisdom that God has waiting for you.

One more encouragement: practice doesn't make perfect, but engaging in spiritual practices will bring peace. In Philippians

4:9, Paul points out that practicing is what creates the space for God's peace to grow within us:

> Keep putting into practice all you learned and received from me—everything you heard from me and saw me doing. Then the God of peace will be with you.

The good news in Paul's teaching is that you have control over deciding to show up. There's much that you can't control, but choosing to learn about these practices and how to live them out is 100 percent in your control.

You show up and God does the rest. To use a popular saying from my family addiction support group: *Keep coming back!*

Envisioning God's Victory over Chronic Stress

Near the end of the movie *Hidden Figures*, NASA mathematician Katherine Johnson, played by Taraji P. Henson, stands next to Al Harrison, played by Kevin Costner, after watching John Glenn's space capsule splash down after orbiting the earth in a harrowing mission. Costner's character asks, "Do you think we'll get to the moon?" Henson's character replies without missing a beat, "We're already there."[8]

That's vision—when you can see beyond all the inevitable problems, processes, and plans that it will take to get to where you want to be.

While you're looking at all the pages of this book and wondering how long it will take, how tough it will be, or how you'll find the time to de-stress your life, God sees you already there. He has already promised it to you, and now it's time for you to see with spiritual vision for yourself.

God already sees your victory, my friend. I want you to see a glimpse of it before you experience it as well.

I love creating hands-on exercises, so at the end of this section, you'll have an opportunity to create a spiritual vision for your less-stressed life that aligns with what God has already promised you. It's my hope that you'll hold on to this vision so that on the days when you wonder if you're getting better or the days when you "lose it" and find yourself losing hope, you remember that God already sees you in the place where you're praying and trusting Him to transform your heart, mind, and body.

As I formulated the idea for this book, most women I talked to had no idea what a stress-free life could look like. Most told me that high levels of stress every day was normal, an acceptable nuisance attached to the business of life. Why is it so easy to see the stress in our lives but not see a life without stress?

God has already declared the vision in many ways throughout the promises He's given us in Scripture. I've selected one of those verses to help you begin to create a vision for what a life free from chronic stress can look like.

> For God has not given us a spirit of fear and timidity, but of power, love, and self-discipline. (2 Tim. 1:7)

Chronic stress is the gift that the spirit of fear and timidity gives to you. It is most definitely not from God. What God wants to give you is more than just a life free from chronic stress; He wants to fill you with His power, love, and self-control, which will not only free you from chronic stress but also enable you to experience God's great adventure of joy and purpose for your life.

Do you know where the spirit of fear and timidity comes from? The main root is Satan, who has come "to steal and kill and destroy" (John 10:10). To be clear, Satan cheers whenever you worry that your overwhelm will be the end of you because he knows that your continued stress responses will wear down and destroy your body, limiting or even eliminating your effectiveness for the kingdom of God. You weren't created to be a victim of overwhelm. Jesus died and declared that through Him, no matter what you're facing, you've already overcome!

Would you like to "see" what your life would look like as an overcomer? The following exercise casts a vision for what winning the battle against overwhelm will look like for you.

Practical Exercise: Spiritual Vision for Your Journey

Faith is believing in advance what you can't see now. Your faith doesn't need to be based on doing everything in this book or trying harder. Step into this vision with your faith in God, in His power, His promises, and His vision for your victory.

To set this vision into motion, I have adapted 2 Timothy 1:7 with some spaces and prompts for you to begin seeing and praying for God to lead you to the place where you find freedom from chronic stress and everything associated with it.

For God has not given _____
(your name)

a spirit of fear over _____
(what is stressing you out?)

and timidity about _____
(what is holding you back
from this experience?)

but of power to _____
(what do you need God's supernatural
power to do in your life or situation?)

74

and love to _____

> (how would your life be different if you had less
> stress and more time to invest in others?)

and self-discipline to START _____

> (healthy God-honoring
> attitudes or behaviors)

and to STOP _____

> (unhealthy stress feelings, physical effects,
> or unhealthy habits)

SO THAT _____

> (what kind of dream would you like to live
> out in your life, your family, your church,
> your community, or the world?)

God, with You all things are possible. Today, we pray for Your spiritual vision for our lives. You've already promised my sister victory over the chronic stress that has claimed her life for way too long. Prepare her now to receive the stress-busting gifts of Your power, love, and self-control. As a special request, God, give her a glimpse of the great adventure of joy and purpose that You have for her life on the other side of this experience to encourage her along the journey ahead. In Jesus's name, amen.

6

GOD, I CAN'T BUT YOU CAN, SO I WILL LET YOU

SURRENDER

> While it looks like things are out of control, behind the scenes there is a God who hasn't surrendered His authority.
>
> A. W. Tozer

We wouldn't feel stressed if everything in life went according to plan, right? If we knew how to stop our kids from making disastrous decisions or how to handle that one person at church who acts like your business is their business, our heartbeats would stay steady, and we wouldn't have to manage our stress response.

Since life happens, stress will happen. Winning the battle of overwhelm isn't about eliminating all the stressors from your life; it's about enlarging your view of God and increasing your connection to Him. As God's strength makes you stronger than your stress, you discover the blessing of peace instead of overwhelm in your circumstances.

Giving God space to work in your life begins with the first spiritual practice that we'll tackle together: surrender. This is a practice that scared me the most for years because, even though I was stressed, surrender requires that I do things that make me feel more powerless and therefore even more stressed. Yet this practice has been the door to the peace that passes all understanding, and it's my go-to practice whenever I sense overwhelm creeping in and don't know what to do.

Surrender is giving over to God what is out of your control by placing it into His control and allowing Him to determine what's best.

The spiritual practice of surrender is the cornerstone practice that the other practices are built upon. Unless you open your hands in surrender to God, you can't receive what He is waiting to give to you through the other practices. God is a giving God, but He doesn't force His gifts on us. Surrender is an act of trust between you and God. By trusting God, you believe that He will show up and do what is best for you.

There's a lot of misunderstanding about what surrender is, so we'll walk through that together. At the end of this chapter, I'll provide some next steps to help you begin practicing surrender in your life.

Paul's Principles of Surrender

The apostle Paul offers powerful and unique encouragement on the practice of surrender that will enlighten our journey and practice. At the start of his letter to the Philippian church, Paul makes several statements that highlight some principles of surrender that allowed him to experience the powerful peace of God that he would write about later in that same letter.

1. Paul never forgets that God's power and sovereignty are always at work.

And I am certain that God, who began the good work within you, will continue his work until it is finally finished on the day when Christ Jesus returns. (Phil. 1:6)

Here Paul writes how God is always at work within us as believers. He cares about your circumstances, but His top priority is His eternal plan regarding your soul and your salvation. God will use your circumstances to accomplish His eternal plan, but He isn't hung up on your circumstances, because God knows how good His plan is for you (Jer. 29:11).

Even as he's chained in prison, Paul believes that God is on the throne and active in carrying out His eternal plan. Imagine practicing surrender while sitting in a prison cell. Paul has no idea from one day to the next what will happen in his life. Some of you feel this way today. What brings Paul peace is remembering that God is active and attentive, even when Paul's circumstances seem to indicate differently. Paul writes that God's work won't finish until Jesus comes back, and that reminder serves us well. We can't expect life to be problem-free until eternity.

2. Our character is more important to God than our circumstances.

For I want you to understand what really matters, so that you may live pure and blameless lives until the day of Christ's return. (Phil. 1:10)

If it weren't for our struggles, most of us wouldn't draw close to God. Even now, as I write this chapter on surrender, I've had to let go of something dear to me that I couldn't control over the weekend. It would be easy for me to let this circumstance spread across my entire world, but there's nothing I can do to change it.

Rather than obsessing about what I could have done or if there is anything I could still do, I can choose to live in the moment like Jesus did. Jesus practiced forgiveness, grace, and mercy, so when I let go of my situation, I can do the same. That's where I experience God's peace.

It's easy for us to lock in on what's missing, broken, or changed in our lives and make that our focus from sunup to sundown. However, in Philippians 1:10, Paul tells the believers to center their lives on developing Christlike character. Whatever is big in your world right now, is it time for you to bring it back down in size and instead center on Jesus? What about Jesus's character can you apply to your situation?

3. Paul doesn't take all of his problems personally.

Those others do not have pure motives as they preach about Christ. They preach with selfish ambition, not sincerely, intending to make my chains more painful to me. But that doesn't matter. Whether their motives are false or genuine, the message about Christ is being preached either way, so I rejoice. And I will continue to rejoice. (Phil. 1:17–18)

Here's a reason why I admire Paul: while he was in prison, preachers jumped in and started preaching to the people Paul had previously discipled. The preachers were there to capitalize on the foundation that Paul had laid, and not only that—their motives were selfish.

If I were Paul in prison, I'd be livid. I'd have my pencil and paper ready to send letters in hopes of blocking the preachers. Not Paul. He let it go. Paul doesn't care about their motives; if they preach the gospel of Jesus, he will rejoice. He doesn't let their issues create a problem for him.

Some of us are carrying stress because we've wrongly assumed that something was our fault when we had nothing to do with it. Yes, it may cause you pain, but suffering comes in when you take it personally and let your self-esteem or confidence suffer because of it.

QTIP (Quit Taking It Personally) is a favorite slogan of mine because it reminds me that whatever someone else is doing usually has nothing to do with me. This is the slogan that you apply when someone does something that hurts you, but they were acting out of their own pain, selfishness, or wrong beliefs. Remind yourself that the actions of others do not determine your response. Keep your eyes on Jesus and keep good boundaries.

4. Paul holds his life loosely.

For to me, living means living for Christ, and dying is even better. (Phil. 1:21)

Years ago, I had just finished up a women's conference in Central America when two gangs with guns and automatic weapons opened fire on each other in the neighborhood where I was staying. Our host directed us under the beds as the sounds of bullets filled the air.

As I lay under the bed, I pecked out a message on my tablet to my family back home. I realized that there was nothing stopping a random bullet from ending my life. It was then, under that bed, that I had to make peace with God's ultimate control over my life. I've held on to that during other stressful times, including another shootout, healthcare scares, and each time I travel. There's a peace that comes with putting your life in God's hands and leaving it there.

In Philippians 1:21, an imprisoned Paul, who had no idea what his future would hold, declares, "For to me, living means living for Christ, and dying is even better." He admits being torn between which one he wants more, but his willingness to hold both outcomes in tension and not tie himself to the expectation of one or the other brings Paul peace.

5. Paul remembers that he is a citizen of heaven.

We are in this struggle together. You have seen my struggle in the past, and you know that I am still in the midst of it. (Phil. 1:30)

Since he knew that earth was not his permanent home, Paul didn't let himself spin on earthly matters that had no eternal consequence. Paul lived by the culture of his permanent home, heaven. He told the believers to not be intimidated by their enemies because those troublemakers have an expiration date. Finally, since the body of Christ is a family, Paul reminded the believers that "we are in this struggle together," and that camaraderie provided much-needed support, especially as Paul was cut off from the other believers while in prison.

As citizens of heaven, you and I can look at our temporary home and rather than seeing every news report, social decline, or political upheaval through the eyes of gloom and doom, these moments can be reminders that God has something better waiting for us one day.

These are surrender mindset lessons for Paul. Take a moment to choose one or two to reflect upon. In the next section, you'll learn how to begin your practice of surrender.

What Is God Calling You to Surrender?

In your room of spinning plates, chances are there's one plate that you obsess over. This is the plate that you hover by, pace around, and at times panic about more than the others. You've

81

been known to lose sleep by spinning this plate in your thoughts, plotting how to keep the plate spinning even though you have other matters in your life to attend to. You might be exhausted, but you are convinced in your bones that by hook or by crook, you're going to keep that plate on its pole.

Here's a kicker: it might not even be your plate. I speak from a lifetime of experience on this.

For a decade, my spinning plate was keeping my family together even though addiction was slowly breaking us apart. I'm not arguing that family plates aren't good and worthy plates to keep spinning, but this time my family was spinning on a pole of addiction. For years, I obsessed over my spinning plate of family because I believed that it was all on me to keep it from falling. When that plate fell off, I jumped right in to pick it up, glue it back together, and do whatever I could to put it spinning again. I focused on the plate, not God. My spins were not in faith but fear. I was good at fear spins. What does a fear-driven spin look like? In my Bible study *Surrendered: Letting Go and Living Like Jesus*, I write about the SHINE control-loving behaviors:[1]

Stonewalling—digging in one's heels without listening or being unwilling to work as part of a team

Helicoptering—micromanaging others

Interrupting—interfering when someone is speaking or inserting oneself into another's plans

Nagging—repeating instructions with a harassing tone

Excessive Planning—obsessing over details in hopes of a certain outcome

These are the tools that I pulled out whenever I sensed any threat to my family. I was a warrior who wanted to protect what I loved, fix what was broken, and try to move my out-of-control situation back on track. I believed that the sleepless nights, constant racing heart, and frequent anxious tears were worth it because I was fighting for something important, something that I believed God loved and honored too. For years, my fear and I spun that plate and I prayed that God would keep things going. The problem was that I prioritized my actions over trusting God.

And then one day I threw a lot of dishes through my kitchen window.

It's not our situation that causes our stress but our unwillingness to let go of control of the situation. Remember, stressors are the people, places, and things in our lives, but our stress is our reaction to our situation, not the situation itself.

Surrender is letting go of the belief that you're responsible for fixing a situation or forcing a desired outcome. It's a spiritual practice because surrender requires the rewiring of your will or your determination about how you believe life should be. I believed that God loved families, so I believed that He would keep my family together. Before surrender, the only outcome that I would accept was the picture I had in my mind. I used the control-loving behaviors to push for my preferred outcome. I believed that fighting for my family was a good hill to die on. The problem was that my fighting strategy was based on my ideas of how I thought things should go. My attempts to fix and to force solutions led to chaos, not peace or my desired outcome. It took my willingness to admit that I wasn't in control and to let go of the picture in my mind. Only then did I finally experience God's perfect peace.

Whatever is out of control in your life right now isn't out of God's control. The question is whether you'll stop your attempts to control it. It's scary though. When we tell God that He's in control, that means He will handle our situation differently than we had planned and on a timetable that will be much slower and much more frustrating than if we attempt to take care of it ourselves.

Yet, surrender is our only path to peace.

Without surrender, you're bringing a squirt gun to a gunfight. God is contending for an eternal purpose while you're fighting to fix a particular situation or hoping to set up future success or comfort.

The practice of surrender equips you to give over and place into God's hands whatever you love or want to fix or change and then leave it there. Once it's out of your hands, then God fills your hands with His peace. His peace allows you to live out His eternal purpose for you while He's working through your situation. God's peace protects you from getting worn down and worn out by worry, not taking care of yourself, and feeling hopeless if the outcome isn't as you'd hoped.

When I reflected on Paul's encounter with the risen Jesus on the road to Damascus in Acts 9, what I found interesting was Paul's immediate surrender of his agenda. He was on his way to an important mission, and he let it all go instantly. While his blindness after his encounter with Jesus was partly to blame, Paul could have ordered his companions to bring him to Damascus and then told them to go look for the Christians. Instead, Paul stopped what he was doing and followed Jesus's instructions. He just stopped.

Have you sensed God telling you to stop? As you think about that stressful situation in your life, consider those SHINE control-loving behaviors and which ones you might be using. Here's the big question: What are you afraid will happen if you stop?

As I write these words, I know that some of you are worried about children with mental health issues or spouses who've been unfaithful or the possibility of losing your home or of facing the future unmarried and alone.

But do you have peace right now?

In my family addiction support group meeting, we have table tents with the slogan "Pain is inevitable. Suffering is optional."

In this context, suffering is the emotional distress or stress that we experience when we don't let go of control. Suffering comes in the form of "what if" worries and wringing our hands. I fear that some of you are experiencing suffering on top of your stress.

God can give you peace. Are you willing to surrender?

There are principles when it comes to practicing surrender that you can use today. As you implement these principles, you'll learn how to make room for God to pour His power into your situation and give you His peace.

Starting Your Spiritual Practice of Surrender

One of the most well-known spiritual exercises is Richard Foster's "palms down, palms up."[2] I'm using his simple instructions, but I've scripted the prayers.

1. Begin with your palms down. Start with prayer. If you need words, you can use these:

> *God, I give _____ to You because it is weighing down my mind or causing overwhelm. I release my fear of _____. I release using control-loving behaviors like _____ to force a solution or direct the outcome.*

2. Take a few deep breaths and then turn your palms up.

> *God, I would like to receive Your promises. I recognize Your presence with me right now. I would like to receive Your peace about _____. I would like to receive Your patience with/for _____. I trust You with the outcome. Amen.*

Here is another practical exercise to support your spiritual practice of surrender:

1. On the inside back cover of this book, write down two or three verses that remind you of God's power, love, and eternal plan and letting go of control. Leave a space between each verse. In that space draw a line with a star in front of it.
2. On the line with the star, write down a personalized statement, which we'll call strength statements. For example, "I believe that God . . ." or "I trust God to . . ."
3. Each day, begin your prayer time with reviewing those verses and declaring your trust in God.
4. When you feel stressed, write down everything that you are stressed about on a separate sheet of paper. Put a mark by what you can't control.
5. Put that list in your open palms and recall what you know about God and what you believe from your strength statements.
6. Pray over the problem or circumstance you hold in your hand, starting with your strength statements, and then pray this prayer of surrender: *God, I can't but You can, so I will let You.*

7

LETTING GOD WORK WHILE YOU REST

SABBATH

You can pretend like the need for rest somehow does not apply to you and your life, but your yawn tells a different story.

Dr. Saundra Dalton-Smith

Every seasoned parent and childcare worker knows that moment when a toddler needs a nap. That kid is having a great time but then with no provocation begins whining, then starts to get unreasonable before falling onto the floor. Once the kid crosses the line over to cranky, there is no such thing as a rational conversation. The only solution is rest.

We may have jobs, driver's licenses, and homes, but we aren't much different from toddlers. We bounce from one activity to the next all day long. At some point, we start feeling cranky. *Is it time to go home yet? I don't want to answer another phone call from a dumb customer! Why can't someone cook for me tonight?* Like a car's gas tank gets empty, our energy level diminishes throughout the day. Instead of taking ourselves to rest or to bed, we do the opposite. We keep pushing to the next task or obligation. We know that rest is important, but there are too many other urgent matters requiring our attention. "Running on empty" becomes the vibe of our life. We just keep going and going. A 2014 Stanford University study on work reported that our productivity decreases once we work more than fifty hours a week.[1] Yet, we wear our long hours like a beaten-up badge of honor.

If you cock your head and listen carefully, you'll likely hear God whispering: *Stop. Sit. Rest.*

God knows that you aren't lazy. He sees you doing the best that you can. You're running from one spinning plate to the next, sometimes stretching yourself to spin multiple plates at a time. Each morning, your body begs for more sleep. Your achy muscles ask you to reconsider getting up. Your aching head implores you to stop thinking in circles so that it can try to catch up. You feel the ache in your heart as it grinds to shift gears from one emotional situation to the next. Imagine your heart hunched over and out of breath with its elbows on its knees, saying, "I love you, but I'm not sure how much more I can take"?

We ghost our body's requests for a break because we believe that it's more noble to push ourselves for the sake of our families or to work for a better future. Humanity's collective toxic trait is the belief that recovery after exhaustion is better than resting to prevent exhaustion.

God disagrees.

God knows that when we're tired, we're vulnerable to increased stress and the temptation of sin. From a physical perspective, God also knows that at a certain point our bodies will go on strike and shut down. This is known as burnout. Unfortunately, the physical, emotional, and relational cost to get the body back to work is high.

The spiritual practice of Sabbath is learning how to stop living in constant motion so we can see where God is moving on our behalf. The bottom line for this spiritual practice is that we are blessed when we rest.

In a world where we judge our worth by our productivity, Sabbath, a word that means "cessation,"[2] is a reminder that we are God's creation. He understands our limited human capacity. Resting is a tool that God has designed to bless you in every area of your life. Sabbath rest isn't a multilevel marketing opportunity in which millions participate but only a few reach the top level. God created Sabbath, and everyone who engages in it experiences God's best blessings.

Maybe you're thinking, *But what will happen to my life if I pause for Sabbath?*

It might seem like full-on irresponsibility to stop spinning your plates for a day, but wearing yourself out day after day isn't smart either. If you want to win the battle of overwhelm, Sabbath is a key weapon. I appreciate the wisdom of Rebekah Lyons: "We cannot run if we cannot rest."[3]

There are four blessings that you experience through the spiritual practice of Sabbath:

1. The blessing of allowing your body to replenish its resources instead of draining them.
2. The blessing of letting your mind rest. Since there is less doing and problem-solving, this should result in fewer perceived threats and fewer triggers for any fight-or-flight responses.
3. The blessing of investing in relationships that are often neglected because of exhaustion, hurry, and stress.

4. The blessing of undoing wrong beliefs attached to using work to prove our worthiness or fears associated with questioning God's provision.

These four truths regarding the spiritual practice of Sabbath are helpful for you to know and hopefully will challenge you to incorporate rest into the weekly rhythm of your life.

Sabbath Has God's Stamp of Goodness

In the very first chapter of Genesis, right at the beginning of the Bible, we read about God's important work in creating the world. Great detail is given not only to what was created but also to God's declaration of approval over the work that He'd done. Read Genesis 1 and notice how each day's work is detailed.

Most of us know what it's like to wake up with a demanding to-do list, but we've never had a to-do list like God's:

Day Three:
1. Sort the land and seas.
2. Make stuff grow. Include the seeds so more stuff can grow later.
3. Add in different kinds of varieties just for kicks. Do the extra fun stuff too.

If you ask me, God was on a hot streak when He invented avocados, mangos, pineapples, and brussels sprouts. Yes, you heard that right. I said brussels sprouts. They are so good. God said so.

Even more profound than the wonder of God's creation is that God already knew the world He created would moan under the weight of humanity's bad choices, carelessness, rebellion, and sin, yet He didn't let that stop Him from taking satisfaction in the goodness of the work that He'd completed.

In Genesis 2:2, we read that on the seventh day God rested. He didn't give any reasons for resting. He didn't need to justify rest or let everyone know that He'd be back hard on the grind the next day. He rested. Period. Was God done with His work as the sovereign God of the universe? No. There was more work to do, but He reached a point and paused.

One of the clues that we see in Scripture is the practice of *Shabbat*, which is the Hebrew word for Sabbath. Historically, the practice has its roots before God gave the command to Moses at Mount Sinai. Practically speaking, Shabbat is observed from sunset on Friday until sundown on Saturday.

While there's no hard rule that your Sabbath must be on Saturday, this is a good starting point if you need to establish a place in your life to create a stopping point. I worked for my church for years and we had weekend services on Saturday as well as Sunday, so Sabbath on Saturday didn't work for me. My Sabbath began Thursday night through my day off on Friday.

God gave Moses the Ten Commandments and included a requirement to observe a Sabbath day. It is a command. God was just as serious about rest as He was about the other commandments such as honoring one's father and mother and not committing murder.

In the New Testament, even though the Jewish religious leaders had added legalistic rules to the practice of Sabbath, that didn't take away from its God-given goodness. Jesus affirmed the Sabbath as good when He declared that it was made for us as humans, while simultaneously calling out the religious leaders for weighing the day down with traps and laws (Matt. 12:1–14; Mark 2:23–28; Luke 6:1–11).

Sabbath Is a Gift

They must realize that the Sabbath is the LORD's gift to you.
(Exod. 16:29)

When the Israelites escaped Egypt after four hundred years of captivity, their habits and mindsets were carved into slavery beliefs of scarcity, fear, and exhaustion. Generations of Israelites were born, lived, and died in the daily cycle of scrapping for their survival, with limited choices and in constant fear for their well-being and safety.

As they entered the wilderness, part of God's plan was to break that cycle of stress and fear. After they complained about the lack of food, God began feeding them manna from heaven, and it's here that we witness God teaching the Israelites how to practice Sabbath.

Exodus 16 records God's instructions for the people to gather manna each morning. They were to collect only as much as they needed for that day, and God made sure that everyone had enough. On the sixth day, however, they were to gather twice as much, as God's provision came with a blessing and one specific instruction:

> They must realize that the Sabbath is the LORD's gift to you. That is why he gives you a two-day supply on the sixth day, so there will be enough for two days. On the Sabbath day you must each stay in your place. Do not go out to pick up food on the seventh day. (v. 29)

God wanted to bless His people with the gift of rest, but He knew that a weekly practice was needed to break their slavery mentality so that they could receive the blessing.

Think about this from God's perspective: He'd proven throughout the week that He could take care of His people by sending actual food from heaven. Unlike during their years of slavery, the Israelites didn't have to hustle to survive, they only needed to pick up the food. They didn't need to fear where the food was coming from or stress out about whether there would be enough. However, when Moses told the people to not save the manna overnight because there would be fresh manna in the morning, their scarcity fears kicked in at first and some of them disobeyed. The next morning their manna was spoiled. They performed the extra work and it went to waste.

Here's an interesting thought: How many times have you overworked and you never reaped the benefit of that work because it spoiled your relationships or your health? Rotten manna is an unnecessary waste that you can avoid.

We see the gift of the Sabbath in God's instructions for the people to gather food for six days and then take a break on the seventh day. This was not optional. God commanded His people to rest. He needed them to be still, to undo for a day so that they could stop and see that God was taking care of them and they didn't have to stress about how to take care of themselves.

God's gift of a weekly Sabbath also gave them the opportunity to undo generations of trauma from years spent living in the tyranny of slavery. Families had an opportunity to spend time together and connect. People had time to allow their bodies to heal both physically and mentally. As a community, they could meet to give thanks to God and share stories of how He took care of them.

Take a moment and think about what you're able to do when you are rested.

- You can make better decisions and follow through on them.
- You have more creativity.
- You have more energy to pour into your relationships, marriage, and friendships.

Imagine waking up one day each week and looking forward to unhurried, unpressured time with the people in your life. Could Sabbath be God's built-in provision for the ripping-and-running pace of your family life? Think about one day a week when, instead of yelling for your family to hurry up or only communicating with them to give out chore assignments, you could look your family members in the eye and say, "Tell me more about that work project, honey," or ask, "How can I encourage you more?" Sabbath is an invitation to connect and make memories. Sabbath gives me a chance as a single person to reach out to friends that I'm too busy to see during the week. I also have time to call my adult kids and extended family to see how they are doing. Sabbath is a relational gold mine if we take advantage of it.

As you begin your Sabbath practice, you'll also learn that you don't need to spin your plates as often as you think. Trust me, there will be a day when you discover that God is taking care of some of those plates, and even though you've been spinning them, He doesn't need you to. This knowledge will build your trust that God is showing up for you and cares for you. You don't have to wear yourself out or work so hard, my friend.

For me, mental rest is one of the top selling points for Sabbath. Sabbath sets us up for better sleep throughout the week, and when we sleep better, our brains are more efficient and work better.

I believe that all of us can see ourselves in the Israelites' struggle to accept Sabbath as a gift from God. I hope that you will grasp that gift because He has already given it to you.

Sabbath Is an Expression of Grace

> Then Jesus said to them, "The Sabbath was made to meet the needs of people, and not people to meet the requirements of the Sabbath." (Mark 2:27)

If grace is undeserved favor from God that we don't have to earn, then Sabbath is God's weekly reminder of His grace. This is a day that God wants you to receive with joy! At the start of your practice, you might feel uneasy or distracted by what's not getting done. You might even feel guilty because working is how you prove your worth.

That hit a nerve, didn't it?

Sabbath is a spiritual practice that reminds us that God loves and cares for us as human beings, not human doings. So many of us are working so hard to prove our value or to invalidate someone else's judgment of us, or as a form of control because we've felt helpless in other areas of our lives.

God commands you to practice experiencing His peace in learning to just be. He knows that as you practice this each week, you'll undo those wrong beliefs that drive your overworking, which can contribute to your overwhelm.

You are not what you do. You are, however, a child of God.

Time stops for no one, but Sabbath holds within it a slowness that blesses you in delightful ways. When you have an entire day without needing to think about a schedule, a to-do list, or the pressure to compete, time slows in the most delicious of ways. You may not experience this at first as you watch the clock and think about all you could be doing. But the more you practice Sabbath, you'll come to experience the grace of slowing down time and the freedom from the hurry sickness that causes so much stress.

For me, Sabbath is a grace that gives me time to catch my breath, to let my muscles relax. I have time to reflect and linger. I can read books or stare out the window. By undoing, Sabbath restores what I lose during the week.

This becomes a grace that you'll learn to carry with you throughout the week. Once you adjust to the rhythm of Sabbath, the benefits of connecting with others, caring for yourself, and engaging with God multiply exponentially. It's a lot easier to navigate your life of spinning plates when you know that you've got a plan to rest up before you return to spinning them.

Practicing Sabbath Stillness

Establishing a weekly rest day will take time to settle into. However, if you are obedient to God's command, He will help you with any unique hiccups. Rather than create rules for Sabbath, here are some guiding principles for personalizing your own Sabbath practice. To help you remember, use the acronym ESPN.[4]

E—Enjoy Engaging with God and Others

Approach your practice of Sabbath with anticipation and joy. After all, it is a gift from God, not a trap to set you up for failure. Release your fears and concerns about certain scenarios to God. If He has gifted Sabbath to you, then He will reveal a solution.

S—Suspend Appointments and Obligations

This is the one day when you don't schedule anything on your calendar, nor do you plan for housework or errands. The goal is not only to keep your body from rushing around but also to let your mind rest.

Lots of questions about Sabbath arise from parents and caregivers. Caring for children and loved ones doesn't break the Sabbath, but the care should not include shuttling them to sports games and doctor's appointments, doing chores, or problem-solving. This is a day for you to be present and invest in the people you love with your time and attention.

P—Plan Ahead

Be intentional about creating time with God to reflect on His goodness to you in the previous week. Plan whether you want to do this in prayer, by journaling, or on a walk.

Set yourself up for success by planning your meal the night before, cleaning up the parts of your home where you will spend your Sabbath, making plans to enjoy the day, and having a conversation with your family or loved ones about how to enjoy Sabbath together. Everyone will get excited if you explain that it's a rest day rather than a workday!

One of my favorite examples of planning ahead comes from Jewish author Tiffany Shlain, who wrote *24/6: The Power of Unplugging One Day a Week*. In her family, they make the same meal every Friday, but they invite different people over to share their Shabbat dinner. They also begin their meal by inviting everyone around the table to share a blessing. Everyone has a card with a word on it like love, humility, or strength, and they are asked to share what it means to them. Shlain's family uses the same format every week, but they experience the richness and variety of new voices around their table.[5]

N—No Electronic Dependence

Devices aren't evil, but they can be a distraction and undermine the blessings that God wants you to experience on the Sabbath. A study conducted in 2017 revealed that the use of laptops by students in a classroom distracts everyone—not just the people using them![6]

Your devices can be used on the Sabbath if they don't interfere with the overall goal of making space for you to receive from God.

If you need more practical guidance, you can put all your devices in a basket and place them in a cabinet for the day. Shlain also says that her family keeps a landline phone, so they can put their devices away on Shabbat but people can still get in touch with them if needed.

8

TALKING TO GOD

PRAYER

The most important purpose of prayer may be to let our
true selves be loved by God.

Philip Yancey

The spiritual practice of prayer is regularly communicating with
God through the spoken word, meditating, and listening. Like
any important relationship, prayer is a means of deepening
our connection with God and building trust by learning more
about God.

When you have a spiritual practice of prayer, you invite
the supreme God into the deepest, dearest, and even darkest places of your inner self. As the psalmist wrote long ago,
"Search me, O God, and know my heart" (Ps. 139:23). But
the spiritual practice of prayer isn't one-sided. Prayer draws

us closer to the heart of God so that we know Him better as well. In his classic book *How to Listen to God*, Charles Stanley explains why God created prayer for us to engage with Him: "He wants us to know the truth about Himself . . . to grasp His majesty, His holiness, His power, His love, His grace, and His joy."[1]

By its very nature, overwhelm is opposed to the practice of prayer. I'm not saying that an overwhelmed person doesn't pray. Overwhelm tries to convince you that there is no room in your heart to pray or no words for you to pray with. For most people who are overwhelmed, prayer becomes a last resort instead of a proactive spiritual practice that opens space for connection, intimacy, and a chance to receive from God.

Ever wondered why it might be physically difficult for you to pray when you are feeling overwhelmed? One day you're running late to work and the school calls while you're driving to the office—one of your kids is sick and you need to turn around and pick them up. As you circle back to the school while watching the clock and wondering what to do with a sick kid while you're at work, someone from your job calls to tell you that there is a client waiting for you and to hurry up. Undone by the overwhelm of too much at once, you toss your hands up in the air at a stoplight, and when you bring them back down, you tip your coffee all over yourself and your clothes.

Insert frustrated scream here.

In the space of five minutes, everything in your life is a mess. Now those overwhelm thoughts trigger your body's stress response. All of a sudden, you can't think of any words to pray. Oh no! Does this mean that you don't trust God or there is something wrong with your faith? You feel like you literally cannot pray. What's going on?

There's a reason this happens, and it has nothing to do with your level of faith. Ready to revisit fight-or-flight again?

Years ago, I worked as a pharmaceutical sales representative, and I sold one of the top antidepressants in the world for anxiety and panic disorder. As part of the training, I learned how God designed our brains to work, specifically the different hormones in our brains and what happens when there are hormonal imbalances due to trauma, stress, or anxiety.[2]

Have you ever heard of an "amygdala hijack"? Daniel Goleman, bestselling author of *Emotional Intelligence*, coined that phrase to describe how your amygdala, that part of the brain that keeps track of your emotional memories, can take over before you can think rationally about a situation. Therefore, you might start panicking when overwhelmed and have a hard time figuring out what you need to do.[3]

Does this mean that your emotions will always hijack your attempts to pray? Absolutely not. The same solution applies that we covered in an earlier chapter. The way to de-trigger your fight-or-flight response is to slow your heart rate down, which sends a message to your body that it is not in danger. Hint: you can start by visiting the Breathing Room. Once your heart rate returns to normal, you should find that your thinking brain can reengage, and you can start intentional problem-solving instead of impulsive, fear-driven reactions.

What does this look like in real time? Paul and his traveling companion, Silas, demonstrated these two factors when they ran into trouble while preaching in Philippi.

Growing up, the apostle Paul would have been taught to pray three basic prayers throughout the day. Paul would have an established practice of prayer. After Paul met Jesus on the road to Damascus, his prayers were no longer attached to fulfilling the requirements of the law; rather, his prayers arose from a desire to connect with God. On his missionary journeys, Paul would share the gospel and he would teach people principles around practicing prayer:

Pray in the Spirit at all times and on every occasion. Stay alert and be persistent in your prayers for all believers everywhere. (Eph. 6:18)

Devote yourselves to prayer with an alert mind and a thankful heart. (Col. 4:2)

On his second missionary journey as recorded in Acts 16, Paul traveled to the city of Philippi, a Roman colony located in modern-day Turkey. On the Sabbath, Paul and Silas left the city to walk down by the river because they hoped that there would be a group of people meeting to pray. Paul and Silas met a woman named Lydia, a successful businesswoman. She listened to Paul preach and accepted Jesus Christ. Not only that, but Lydia invited the missionaries back to her home to be her guests, and she was instrumental in leading her household to Christ.

Trouble eventually found Paul and Silas during their stay in Philippi. On their way to meet more believers for prayer, they encountered a young girl possessed by a demonic spirit. The girl was being trafficked by a group of men who made money off her fortune-telling abilities. At first, it seemed like the girl was cheering on Paul and Silas's work, but they recognized that she was under the influence of an evil spirit. Day after day, the young girl shouted her false words of support, until at one point Paul became frustrated and commanded the evil spirit to come out of her.

Once freed, the young woman was no longer able to tell fortunes and could no longer make money for her captors. In retaliation, her captors dragged Paul and Silas before the authorities where they lied about Paul and Silas's activities, claiming they had committed illegal acts. After a mob of people joined in the protest, the two men were thrown into prison where they were severely beaten and detained in an interior dungeon with their feet shackled.

If I had been in Paul and Silas's position, I'd be overwhelmed with emotion and fear. All they had done was preach the gospel; Paul freed a girl from a demon and they got in trouble. Sometimes, when you think you're doing the best you can and life still backfires on you, it can feel like a wave of disappointment and discouragement, right?

Imagine how fast Paul and Silas's hearts must have raced as the girl's captors grabbed them and dragged them before the authorities. If you've ever had a police car pull up behind you, chances are you know the experience of feeling your heart race.

As they sat in prison, what did Paul and Silas do next? Here's what happened:

Around midnight, Paul and Silas were praying and singing hymns to God, and the other prisoners were listening. (Acts 16:25)

One could argue that Paul and Silas defaulted to prayer because they were overwhelmed and had no other option. Sometimes we pray because we've tried everything else first. But rather than harnessing prayer as a last resort, Paul and Silas prayed first because it was already a practice in their lives. The evidence of this is that Paul and Silas prayed and sang hymns to God, focusing on Him rather than their situation. When prayer is our last resort because we are panicked, we don't tend to be focused on God; we're focused on ourselves.

This may not seem like intentional problem-solving, but it was. Paul and Silas were in prison, and there was no way they would be freed without intervention from God. So prayer was part of their intentional plan instead of panic or fear.

Acts 16 records that there was a massive earthquake and the prison was shaken. This caused the prison doors to fly open, and then supernaturally all the chains of every prisoner fell off. When the jailer thought the prisoners had escaped, he was prepared to end his life. But Paul called out and told him that all the prisoners were still there. Why did the prisoners stay? The answer to that isn't clear, but a few verses earlier we saw how Paul and Silas were praying and singing hymns to God and the other prisoners were listening. Is it possible that amid that difficult and stressful prison environment, the prisoners experienced some supernatural relief to their overwhelm? Maybe they experienced a sense of peace in prison that they knew wouldn't be on the outside of those walls. We don't know, but we do know that because they stuck around, the jailer didn't kill himself. If you read the rest of the account, the jailer cared for Paul and Silas's wounds, and the jailer and those in his household were saved.

Paul and Silas faced overwhelming circumstances, but because they chose to pray first, they did not succumb to the emotional overwhelm.

How can you follow in their footsteps? It's time to get practical about your spiritual practice of prayer.

I'll share nuts-and-bolts tips a little later, but the foundation of a life-giving spiritual practice of prayer requires confidence and consistency.

Confidence

I love it when kids pray. They don't worry about what to say or not say. They just put it out there to God, like this:

Dear God, when will my sister stop being annoying? I'm down to my last patience.

Dear God, thank You for the baby brother, but what I prayed for was a puppy.

We give kids simple instructions around prayer. We tell them that prayer is talking to God. We encourage them to talk to God about whatever they'd like, and we applaud them for any attempts at prayer. While some of what they ask for is silly or nonsensical, we don't discourage kids from praying, because we want to encourage the practice to lead back to a relationship with God.

Confidence in prayer is knowing that God listens to your prayers, cares about your prayers, and answers your prayers according to His sovereignty.

I've spoken with countless believers over the years who struggle with confidence in prayer. Some question whether God is listening because they can't see or hear God communicate back. Others struggle with whether God cares because prayers for healing, rescue, or important dreams haven't been answered.

Yet, even with our questions, God invites us to pray. Pastor and author Max Lucado writes, "Resist the urge to complicate it. Don't take pride in well-crafted prayers. Don't apologize for incoherent prayers. No games. No cover-ups. Just be honest— honest to God. Climb into His lap. Tell Him everything that is on your heart."[4]

If I can speak some encouragement to you today: *God loves you and He wants to hear from you.*

How do you regain confidence in praying so that you can engage in a regular practice of prayer? Here are five reminders to build your trust that your prayer practice matters to God and is meaningful for your life, whether you are overwhelmed or not. I'm pairing these reminders with Scripture since the Bible says a lot about prayer.

1. God cares about your prayers.
   So let us come boldly to the throne of our gracious God. There we will receive his mercy, and we will

find grace to help us when we need it most. (Heb. 4:16)

2. It's okay if you don't always know what to say.
   And the Holy Spirit helps us in our weakness. For example, we don't know what God wants us to pray for. But the Holy Spirit prays for us with groanings that cannot be expressed in words. (Rom. 8:26)

3. Plain and honest is always better than fancy and fake.
   When you pray, don't babble on and on as the Gentiles do. They think their prayers are answered merely by repeating their words again and again. (Matt. 6:7)

4. Prayer is the sign that you want God's help.
   Keep on asking, and you will receive what you ask for. Keep on seeking, and you will find. Keep on knocking, and the door will be opened to you. (Matt. 7:7)

5. Don't give up on prayer, even if you're struggling. Stay open to God's help!
   Never stop praying. (1 Thess. 5:17)

Consistency

Now that you have these reminders from Scripture, let's talk about how to make your prayer practice consistent. The more that you pray, the more likely that you will pray.

Practicing prayer is most successful when it becomes a habit. Here are some practical tools to help, followed by a prayer framework if you need a place to start praying.

1. Find a prayer bestie.

For where two or three gather together as my followers, I am there among them. (Matt. 18:20)

When Jesus taught His disciples how to pray in Matthew 6, He used plural pronouns like "our" and "us." While we can pray on our own, Jesus taught us that prayer is also collective. To practice effective prayer, partner up!

Tell a trusted Christian friend that you desire to be more consistent with prayer and ask her to pray with you once a week. Praying with someone in an established rhythm helps you create consistency and accountability. If you struggle with prayer on your own, having another person to talk to God with you can be helpful. You can exchange prayer requests before you start praying; it's so encouraging to have someone pray with you and for you, especially if life is stressful.

2. Envision yourself as a woman who prays first about everything.

In *Atomic Habits*, James Clear proposes that success in setting up a new habit to be successful begins with establishing the desired identity.[5] In the book, he uses the example of a woman who wanted to quit smoking. Rather than declaring that she was going to quit smoking, she began by telling herself that she was a nonsmoker. Shifting her identity eventually took root, so she stopped doing behaviors that were inconsistent with her old identity.

The same can be applied to prayer. Give yourself a prayer identity as a woman who prays first about everything in your life. As you repeat that identity and then add behaviors to feed that identity, it will aid you in making the habit of prayer stick in your life.

3. Center God in your prayers.

When Jesus taught His disciples how to pray in Matthew 6, He began by centering God: "Our Father." This should be the start of our prayers too. Focusing on God in our prayer practice reminds us that God is bigger than our biggest problems, anxieties, or overwhelm. Some practical ways to center God include beginning by listening to hymns or with giving thanks to God, praying a list of the names of God, or acknowledging God's faithfulness and grace in your life.

4. Keep coming back.

In my family addiction recovery support group, we tell each other to keep coming back. We do that because we know that the journey to recovering from the impact of a loved one's addiction ebbs and flows. Sometimes I hear something at a meeting that becomes an aha moment, and other times I show up because I can relate to others and their presence lifts me. But I miss out on all of that if I don't show up. The same applies to prayer. When you don't pray, you miss out.

Prayer isn't about perfection. It's a commitment that you make to a relationship with God. God is always waiting for you to come back, and He's not going to hold your absence against you.

There are times when you will not want to show up to talk to God because it doesn't seem like anything is happening. Maybe you feel guilt or reluctance because you aren't sure that He cares or listens. When you keep showing up in the space of prayer, it's like coming home every day after work. Whether you have other people in your home or you're single like me, showing up matters in your relationships with others or even with yourself. The more you show up, the more you learn about the other person. You learn that prayer is an exchange that is more than words; it's presence, acceptance, openness, and most of all, love.

5. Pray, but remember that the battle belongs to God.

Since the battle belongs to God, He's sovereign over the timing, the outcome, and everything in between. When you pray, be careful that your prayers for intercession aren't disguised as your demand for God to act in a certain way. Rather, the purpose of prayer in heavy spiritual battle flows along the lines of what Priscilla Shirer wrote in her book *Fervent*: "And because prayer is the divinely ordained mechanism that leads you into the heart and the power and the victory of Christ, He knows you'll remain defeated and undone without it."[6] Prayer is your protection in the midst of the battle, not a tool to strong-arm God into what you want Him to do.

Keep praying, but even more, keep trusting that God will be God.

PRAY Method

There are many helpful methods that can assist you with establishing a practice of prayer. Here is one framework you can follow by praying aloud or writing out your prayer in a journal.

P—Praise
Begin with centering God by remembering who He is, His eternal plan, and His faithfulness.

R—Repent
Tell God about your struggles, sin, and anything else on your heart. Ask for forgiveness and for God's help to turn away from wrong attitudes or behaviors and to live for Him.

A—Ask
Make your requests known to God. Tell Him about everything, big and small.

Y—Yield to God's sovereignty and eternal plan

This is like the opening of the prayer. This is where you say, "Yes, God," and follow Jesus's example of praying, "Not my will, but yours be done." Affirm that you trust God no matter what happens.

9

GOD PROMISED IT, I BELIEVE IT

ENGAGING SCRIPTURE

For the word of God is alive and powerful. It is sharper than the sharpest two-edged sword, cutting between soul and spirit, between joint and marrow. It exposes our innermost thoughts and desires.

Hebrews 4:12

In 2022, the American Bible Society reported that 26 million Americans stopped or almost completely stopped reading their Bibles over the course of the previous year. One year. Lead researcher John Plake admits their team was shocked. "We reviewed our calculations. We double-checked our math and ran the numbers again . . . and again. What we discovered was startling, disheartening, and disruptive."[1]

Without Scripture to lead and guide us, the chaos in our heads can be overwhelming. Our overwhelmed minds are like the Hartsfield-Jackson Atlanta airport, the busiest airport in the world. In 2022, over 93 million people passed through the airport (including me at least a dozen times). Almost a thousand flights arrive and depart per day.[2] Your mind is like that airport, with thoughts coming and going, decisions being considered and confirmed, musings about this or that, and dark thoughts lurking in every crevice. Whether it's painful thoughts or healthy thoughts, problems you can't solve or outright struggles with sin, they all interrupt the busy chaos of your mind. Is it any wonder that there are times in life when you're confused and unable to sort things out?

The reality that God's Word is living and active means that it is a powerful weapon that can cut through the chaos in our head and a beacon of light in our overwhelm. The power of God's Word has a way of slicing through confusion, mixed motives, denial, blind spots, and sin to show us the truth that can set us free (John 8:32).

In a world where we can access any information in seconds, the danger is the expectation that information will at some point equal transformation. Just because we can google a variety of solutions to the problems in our lives doesn't mean that those problems will be solved. You can research every angle in the world about your serious health diagnosis, but you have no control over how your body will respond to treatment or a definite answer on your quality of life three to five years from now. Information is great, but it can't provide the kind of peace in your life that the living and active Word of God can.

The spiritual practice of engaging with Scripture is about finding ways to incorporate God's Word into every area of your heart, mind, actions, and life. The goal of engaging with Scripture is to increase our awareness of the character and love of God. It is not to increase the number of colored pencils we have or how many notes are in our Bible. Those are good things, but they aren't the purpose of this spiritual practice.

In my years as a Bible teacher and leader, I've noticed that when the focus of Bible study swings to how often and how long we study rather than how we study, it's hard for a single verse or chapter to be applied and absorbed into the reader's life. Many have faithfully showed up at Bible study or small group for decades, but in the end their lives remain unchanged or they walk away because God's Word never soaked in enough to make a difference. They never allowed the living and active Word of God to transform them. The spiritual practice of engaging Scripture isn't only opening and closing your Bible at a certain time of day. It's bringing Scripture with you wherever you go and letting its words flow through your life in every situation.

Engagement with Scripture means that you can arm yourself with knowing how to interject the Bible into any area of your life at any time. This can also include meditating on Scripture, which is continuing to think and reflect on what you've read in the Bible.

Instead of limiting your practice to one specific way of sitting at a table or in a chair with your Bible and pen for thirty minutes, there are unlimited options for bringing the Bible into every moment of your everyday life. If you're stuck in traffic while hurrying to pick up the kids from school, you can engage with Scripture by listening to the Bible on audio. If you're pacing the floor at night because you're upset about decisions that your teenager has made, you can write out verses on notecards about God's peace and power. The potency of God's Word isn't limited to your sitting in a chair uninterrupted for thirty minutes while you read. In fact, I'd argue that the living and active Word of God is the exact remedy for our overwhelmed lives.

Think about what you've learned so far about overwhelm. When the brain senses a threat, the body activates its stress responses of fight-or-flight. How many of our perceived threats are fears we have in our mind about the four stress triggers of what's uncertain, unexpected, uncontrollable, and uncomfortable? The good news is that each of the four stress triggers is addressed in Scripture so that when such moments hit and you feel the stress coming on, you can speak God's truth to your stress and let God's power back the stress down.

Here are examples of responses from Scripture for each of these stress triggers. If there is a verse that resonates with you, sit with that verse for a few moments and meditate on what God is saying and the truth that you need to remember. Keep these verses handy for when you need them.

- **Uncertain**

  For I know the plans I have for you," says the Lord. "They are plans for good and not for disaster, to give you a future and a hope." (Jer. 29:11)

  Seek the Kingdom of God above all else, and live righteously, and he will give you everything you need. (Matt. 6:33)

- **Unexpected**

  The faithful love of the Lord never ends! His mercies never cease. Great is his faithfulness; his mercies begin afresh each morning. (Lam. 3:22–23)

  Jesus Christ is the same yesterday, today, and forever. (Heb. 13:8)

- **Uncontrollable**

  I am the Lord, the God of all the peoples of the world. Is anything too hard for me? (Jer. 32:27)

  Jesus looked at them intently and said, "Humanly speaking, it is impossible. But with God everything is possible." (Matt. 19:26)

- **Uncomfortable**

> God is our refuge and strength, always ready to help in times of trouble. (Ps. 46:1)

> Each time he said, "My grace is all you need. My power works best in weakness." So now I am glad to boast about my weaknesses, so that the power of Christ can work through me. (2 Cor. 12:9)

Scriptural Checkup from the Neck Up

Siteefy.com keeps track of internet growth in real time and reports that there are over 50 billion webpages.[3] It is difficult for me to quantify just how much information that statistic represents, but it amounts to a lot of ideas and opinions. Unlike people in Paul's time, we have access to new solutions, technologies, ways of thinking, and possibilities. However, not every idea or solution leads us down healthy, helpful, or holy paths.

Some of us have witnessed people in our lives struggle with a trauma from the past or even a church hurt, and they turn to YouTube or another social platform. They begin listening to someone offering to help, and that distant stranger's influence begins to reshape their way of thinking. On a regular basis, I can go online and see a video from someone I knew from church who once served God with all their heart now saying things like, "I've been rethinking things . . ." or "My beliefs have evolved . . ."

You don't have to look far to see the spirit of confusion in our world today. Long ago, Paul explained why:

> For a time is coming when people will no longer listen to sound and wholesome teaching. They will follow their own desires and will look for teachers who will tell them whatever their itching ears want to hear. (2 Tim. 4:3)

Each person is responsible for their own walk with God, so while we can point our fingers and shake our heads at others, God spoke through the prophet Jeremiah long ago telling us that our hearts are deceitful and can lead us down wrong paths (Jer. 17:9). In a world where feelings are validated more than the truth of God, it's easy for us to be led by our emotions instead of God's Spirit (Gal. 5:18–21). Even for those of us who've walked with Jesus for a long time, it's easy to gloss over a few areas where we might feel the tug of the Holy Spirit because if we're living most of the Christian life right, then we give a pass to our little side sin issues or struggles.

We all need a checkup from the neck up. Me too. So let's look at how the spiritual practice of engaging Scripture does more than help us win the battle of overwhelm. This spiritual practice tethers our hearts and minds to God's truth, love, and wisdom so that He can guide us through life.

In his second letter to Timothy, a young man born to a Greek father and a Jewish mother, Paul warns about false teachers, including those who "act religious" but "reject the power that could make them godly" (2 Tim. 3:5). Those words were written long ago but resonate so strongly today! Paul charges Timothy to be faithful to what he was taught because it laid the path to Timothy's salvation in Christ.

Scrutinize claims of new revelation or critiques of Scripture and you'll see that those new paths don't necessarily lead to Jesus. More often those siren calls lead to self-focused or self-serving agendas that result in spiritual death (see Prov. 14:12). Therefore, Paul scripts out a reminder of Scripture's role in our lives:

> All Scripture is inspired by God and is useful to teach us what is true and to make us realize what is wrong in our lives. It corrects us when we are wrong and teaches us to do what is right.

God uses it to prepare and equip his people to do every good work. (2 Tim. 3:16–17)

In a world where we are overwhelmed by information and overwhelmed by our lives, the Bible is a two-edged sword that cuts through our overthinking, our confusion, and the foolish tug to live our own way, and that enables us to yield ourselves to the Holy Spirit's healing in our lives.

Scripture Teaches Us What Is True

Arguably, the best way to learn about God is from God. The Scriptures are God-breathed, meaning from His Spirit to us. He gave us His Word to make it possible for us to know Him. As Paul writes about how the Scriptures teach us what is true, the truth we need to learn ultimately centers around God. When we learn about God, we will know the truth.

One of the most practical examples I can think of is the book of Proverbs. Its timeless wisdom includes instruction in what is true:

> Trust in the LORD with all your heart;
>   do not depend on your own understanding.
> Seek his will in all you do,
>   and he will show you which path to take. (3:5–6)

> Guard your heart above all else,
>   for it determines the course of your life. (4:23)

While truth is a hotly debated concept in our world today, Jesus never campaigned to compel people to believe that He represented truth. He declared it in John 14:6: "I am the way, the truth and the life." His life unfolds the truth about God, and the Bible records that truth. It is true whether we believe it or not.

Learning God's truth should change how you see the world, how you see yourself, and your perception of your circumstances. In Romans 12:2, Paul explains that when we trust God's truth, our hearts, minds, and souls are transformed.

The teachings of Jesus and the apostle Paul were intended to transform people's lives for the better and for eternity. Better doesn't always mean easier or less painful, but it does mean experiencing God's promises. As you think about the verses that have been meaningful to your life, my hope is that you can see where God wants more for you than from you. If you grew up in an environment where the Bible was taught as a list of ways to avoid God's wrath, then a renewed approach to your spiritual practice is recommended.

When you have a regular spiritual practice of engaging Scripture, you create space for God to embed His best into your life, and then you can carry it wherever you go. God's words aren't just powerful when you're sitting in a chair reading your Bible. The Scriptures can breathe life when you're in the emergency room after your child has been in a car accident or when you realize that your parent can no longer live on their own but you live hours away. God's Word guides you, and when you're facing overwhelm, that guidance will lead you in a direction that gives you confidence and strength for whatever you're facing.

Scripture Awakens Us to What Is Wrong

When I'm feeling overwhelmed, my feelings tell me things like, "You're never going to figure this out" or "Good luck, honey, because this is looking really bad for you." God created us to feel emotions, but that doesn't mean that our emotions are in charge. They are real, but they are not reliable predictors of what is real or true in a given moment. We must admit that there are times when our emotions give us the wrong information about our reality.

One of the things I appreciate about the Bible is that it gives us a front-row seat into the lives of people who lived long before us and how they interacted with God and others. In Romans 15:4, Paul says that "such things were written in the Scriptures long ago to teach us," and there are lots of stories in the Bible that caution us about what not to do. For example:

Don't ignore God's instructions and then lie about it.

Regretfully,
Adam and Eve

When you lie, steal, and trick others—like your family— they may want to get revenge.

You're welcome,
Jacob

The Bible does more than directly instruct us to avoid paths that lead to the death of peace, hope, and relationships, and even to eternal death. The lives of people in the Bible act as mirrors for our own lives as well.

In 2 Timothy 3:16, Paul writes that Scripture makes us "realize what is wrong in our lives." Other translations use the word "conviction," which means that the Bible exposes our wrongdoing. Conviction is an act of the Holy Spirit, who leads us into all truth by pointing out where we are off track (John 16:13). This is different from condemnation, which means that there is no hope, only punishment. For those who place their faith in Jesus, Paul tells us there is no condemnation (Rom. 8:1).

The Holy Spirit convicts us of sin, which is intended to lead us back toward God. Satan condemns us, which beats us up, shames us, and makes us afraid to return to God. It's important for you to know the difference. God's goal is always a loving connection with you, and when you realize you're off track, He always welcomes you back. Satan is looking to stab you in the back.

God wants you to know what is wrong because His goal is for you to live out what is useful, profitable, and beneficial to you. God wouldn't be loving if He didn't let you know that you were going the wrong way.

Scripture Corrects Us with God's New Direction

When your parents told you to do something and you asked why, did they ever respond with, "Because I said so"? It can be frustrating to know that something is wrong or needs to be changed but not know the reason or how to make it right.

When Paul writes that Scripture corrects us, this is different from simply telling us what's wrong. The Bible comes alongside us to lead us back toward God. One example of this is in Matthew 18:15–17 when Jesus teaches about problems in relationships. He offers multiple steps for how to safely navigate confronting someone who has offended us. In my own life, there was a season where I was convinced I was right about a relationship conflict, and I was unwilling to be empathetic or compassionate. Jesus's teaching in Matthew 7:1–5 reminded me not to forget about the plank in my own eye as I pointed out the speck in someone else's eye.

During your spiritual practice of engaging Scripture, there will be times when you'll read a passage and sense God prompting your heart to begin applying that to your life. You don't need to fix it all at once. What I like to do is mark a heart next to that verse in my Bible as a reminder that I need to let God work on my heart in that area. You could do that too or think of another way that would be meaningful for you.

Scripture Teaches Us to Do What Is Right

The final goal of Scripture is training us in righteousness, with the result of letting the Holy Spirit lead our lives (Gal. 5:16). How do we allow the Scriptures to train us in righteousness? By putting the teachings of Scripture into practice!

In my youth, I planned to run hurdles in college. Every day, my coach would demonstrate the techniques and tell me what to do, but my training took place when I pushed my practice hurdle against the fence and did the drills repeatedly. There were times when my form was great and times when my coach corrected me. The key to the process was my choice to show up and apply what I learned.

While engaging with Scripture as a spiritual practice can equip you to win the battle of overwhelm, God's best for you is living a life that is pleasing to Him. This isn't a life of following rules but of yielding to the leading of God's Spirit in you, which Paul tells us will result in the fruit of the Spirit: love, joy, peace, patience, kindness, goodness, faithfulness, gentleness, and self-control (Gal. 5:22–23). These reflect the character of God, and let's be honest—this fruit would be much more welcome than the emotions or outcomes associated with overwhelm.

God never instructs us to do something without telling us how to do it. The Scriptures show us the path to living righteously, but we also need to put it into practice.

Here are some specific ways for you to engage with Scripture:

1. Write out Scripture verses and tape them to your bathroom mirror or other places where you'll read them.
2. Listen to an audio Bible when you're in the car, at the gym, or at night before bed.
3. Read Bible verses with family or friends at mealtimes, over coffee, or before bed, and discuss the Scriptures together.

4. Memorize Bible verses that reflect an area of your life in which you believe God wants to change your heart.

5. Sing! Lots of classic hymns and modern worship songs incorporate Scripture. Find those songs. As you sing, you're engaging with God's Word and worshiping Him too.

6. Use Bible dictionaries, commentaries, and online resources to help you better understand Scripture. Tools such as Logos Bible Software and Biblegateway.com offer great connections to resources.

7. Sign up for an online platform that will email you a Bible verse or Bible study content each morning.

8. If you sign up for a plan to read the Bible in a year or for a guided Bible study, give yourself permission to establish a goal of regular engagement but do not judge your performance by how closely you follow their established timetable. Prioritize commitment, not completion of a specific schedule.

9. Pick one Bible verse from your church's weekly sermon and journal about what the verse taught you about God and how you can apply it to your life.

10. If you'd like a simple framework for doing your own Bible study without a guided Bible study experience, you can use the SOAP method outlined below.

SOAP Study Method

Scripture. Choose a passage of Scripture, whether from a daily reading plan, a devotional, or YouVersion's verse of the day. Take your time reading and allow God to speak to you. When you are done, look for a verse that particularly spoke to you that day and write it in your journal.

Observation. What do you think God is saying to you in this passage? Ask the Holy Spirit to teach you and reveal Jesus to you. Paraphrase this Scripture in your own words and write it down in your journal.

Application. Personalize what you have read by asking yourself how it applies to your life right now. Perhaps it is instruction, encouragement, revelation of a new promise, or correction for a particular area of your life. Write how this passage can apply to you today.

Prayer. This can be as simple as asking God to help you use this passage, or it may be a greater insight into what He may be revealing to you. Remember, prayer is a two-way conversation, so be sure to listen to what God has to say! Now, write it out.

BONUS: If you'd like to test out the SOAP method, here's a verse you can use.

> And now, dear brothers and sisters, one final thing. Fix your thoughts on what is true, and honorable, and right, and pure, and lovely, and admirable. Think about things that are excellent and worthy of praise. (Phil. 4:8)

If you'd like to make sure that you're on the right track, you can go to BarbRoose.com/SOAP to view a sample and download a thirty-day SOAP Scripture list for you.

10

DECLUTTERING THE YESES

SIMPLICITY

> Pick your battles.
> Nope. That's too many battles.
> Put some battles back.
> Pick fewer battles.
>
> Anonymous

I watched a recent advertisement from Microsoft that claims the average person makes up to 35,000 decisions per day,[1] and a substantial number of online sources confirm that data. That number may seem high, but when you think about all the daily decisions you are faced with, from easy to difficult, it may not be too far off. Here are just a few of the things you might need to choose over the course of any given day:

- What to wear
- How to do your hair

- Which chores to fit in before leaving for work in the morning
- What to make for dinner
- Whether to change your teenager's curfew or let them drive with a friend
- The best elder care option for your parents

The more decisions you need to make, the more tired you get. Experts refer to this as "decision fatigue," which is the mental weariness that comes from making too many decisions. Dr. Lisa MacLean, a psychiatrist and chief wellness officer for the Henry Ford Medical System, observes that "the more decisions you have to make, the more fatigue you develop and the more difficult it can become."[2] Tired, table for two? That's for me and you.

When we're feeling stressed, we search our environment for clues or cues to the questions regarding our safety, our security, or our worthiness for love. It's exhausting. The decision I had to revisit dozens of times per day during our family addiction crisis was whether I should stay or if it was time for me to go. Besides that crisis, I still faced all the other regular life decisions, like how my kids were doing, how to manage my emotions, what to make for dinner, and how to lead my team well at work while barely holding my life together. My decisions were affected by stress about making decisions.

What decisions eat up your energy? It doesn't have to be crisis decisions that wear you down. If you're building your dream house, the decisions around fixtures or building materials wear you down. Anyone planning a wedding knows the excitement and fatigue that come with choosing the dress, the bridesmaid dresses, the venue, the food, the photographer, and the honeymoon destination. Others might burn energy debating job options, dinner options, retirement timing, or deeper spiritual decisions such as whether to stay or to leave one's church and wrestling with forgiveness. Making that many decisions, good or bad, has the potential to exhaust or even overwhelm you.

The problem comes in when we accumulate too much in our search for what we believe will help us win at life. Attempting decisions when we own too much, obligate ourselves too often, or shoulder too many problems resembles a game of I Spy. There are hundreds of objects drawn on the board but all crowded together. Our minds search for the fastest solution in order to make sense of our world. When there is too much going on, our brains must spend extra energy, which causes mental fatigue.

The more choices we have, the more complicated our decisions will be. We hesitate to settle for the choice in front of us. *What if there is a better option? What if the next opportunity is the one that is the better value, lasts longer, cleans deeper, is more romantic, has better fuel mileage, makes us look skinnier, holds more?* And on and on. It's one thing to figure out where to store all that we're grabbing, but it's another to ask our minds to constantly chase and look for more.

The Huffington Post conducted a survey in which 84 percent of respondents reported having too much stuff. Of those, over half said that all their stuff was causing them a lot of stress.[3] The inability to organize, clean, or find household items when needed is a source of rising stress. If you've watched shows where people struggle with letting go of their possessions, you've been challenged with the reality that when a person is overwhelmed with stuff, it usually indicates interior feelings of overwhelm and is not rooted in stuff itself.

The goal of spiritual simplicity isn't to strip your life down to one cup, one plate, one kind of shampoo, or a single pair of shoes. *The practice of simplicity is making decisions through the filter of contentment so that your decisions do not distract you or disrupt your connection with God.*

Once you have clarity on how to practice simplicity, whether you're making big decisions or even just at the grocery store, you'll feel the freedom of not being drained by tens of thousands of decisions each day. Whether you reduce the number of decisions or you filter your decisions through the lens of contentment, both strategies can decrease the number of potential stressors that can trigger a stress response.

Simplicity will look different for each person based on the Spirit's leading in our lives. So as you immerse yourself in our conversation about this spiritual practice, remember that it will look different for you than for others.

Finding Freedom from the Stress of "Too Much"

As we explore this spiritual practice, I thought it might be helpful to learn from Paul's experience of simplicity and the spiritual attitude that we need as a cornerstone for practicing simplicity. While it might seem as if our emphasis is on practicing simplicity with our possessions, the bigger picture is that what we own or try to acquire reflects the internal clutter of our needs, desires, aspirations, or problems. Ultimately, the fewer decisions we have to make, the less chance for distraction to overwhelm us.

We need God to help us discern what and how much we should own, and there are three questions we can ask ourselves as we prayerfully listen for God's leading.

Is there anything I own that has become an idol in my life?

An idol is anything that we elevate above our devotion to God. It can be any person, place, or thing that would cause you to resent God if it were taken away. By resentment, I don't mean a natural grieving, like if your car was totaled or your house burned down. I'm talking about the kind of bitterness that you'd feel toward God if you lost your job and the reputation or status that came with it. That would be an indicator of an idol.

The problem with idols is that even though they don't have divine power like God, they do have power over our choices and decisions. If creating a beautiful home has become an idol, then your best energy, money, and time will go into DIY projects, endless scrolling on social media for ideas, or spending extra funds on tweaks and touches. When we glorify or esteem what we own, we're taking that glory away from God, who is the only one who deserves it.

There were times in my life when I turned my kids into idols. I would buy them an excessive number of toys, clothes, and shoes because back then I thought I could measure love with what I purchased. However, as the amount of laundry grew because of all the clothes and the playroom became cluttered because of all the toys, I recognized that my good intentions to show love made me cranky, and I would often fuss at my kids for having to manage the very things I had bought them. Something about that didn't seem right.

The consequence of idol worship is emptiness. God knows that. God told Moses and the Israelites that they were to have no other gods before Him, and the same applies to us today. Why? God knows that anything we idolize can't save us or help us. Only God can. You can have a garage full of your favorite hobby and it can bring you happiness, but can it help you when your life falls apart, when your heart is broken, or when you're experiencing a crisis of faith? One Old Testament prophet wrote, "What good is an idol carved by man, or a cast image that deceives you? How foolish to trust in your own creation—a god that can't even talk!" (Hab. 2:18).

Practicing simplicity includes examining your heart to see if any idols are competing with your affection for and connection to God. Moving an idol out of the place in your heart that is reserved for God usually requires getting rid of the idol. This is a tough decision, but keeping anything around that prevents you from being fully devoted to God will hurt you.

What do I own that is a substitute for what I really want?

As someone who has a history of control-loving behavior, I've noticed that there are some possessions I've accumulated because there were other things in my life that I couldn't have. For example, I couponed for years when stores were honoring double and triple the face value on coupons. As I accumulated a stockpile of toothpaste, deodorant, washing detergent, dish liquid, and other items in a closet, I told myself that my efforts amounted to good stewardship by maximizing the resources God gave me. That sounded true.

The truth is that my stockpile arose from a control-loving behavior because I couldn't stop the advancement of the addiction crisis. But I could create my own insurance against uncertainty and buy a substitute for satisfaction and success. While I felt like I lost the security in my marriage, I substituted for it with a different kind of security in possessions. I also liked the feeling of accomplishment, which is something that I didn't experience in our family crisis. Whenever my real-life situation overwhelmed me, I could retreat into couponing and find relief in going to the store and adding more to my stockpile.

As you look around at your possessions, how much of what you own is a substitute for what you really want? During the pandemic, our kitchen cabinets were extra stocked with food not because there was a food shortage but because we wanted to feel in control instead of feeling fear or scarcity. Are you buying shoes upon shoes because you haven't been able to lose the extra weight but cute shoes make you feel better about yourself? Buying gifts for your grandkids is wonderful, but are you overbuying to compensate for the rocky relationship that you had with your kids? When we own a specific car because we long to be admired or we buy a certain house to satisfy an unfulfilled longing from our past, we'll need to keep feeding that longing because those things will never be enough.

Paul's cure for this was contentment. From his prison cell, Paul wrote to believers in Philippi and explained how he could experience joy instead of overwhelm in these circumstances:

> Not that I was ever in need, for I have learned how to be content with whatever I have. I know how to live on almost nothing or with everything. I have learned the secret of living in every situation, whether it is with a full stomach or empty, with plenty or little. For I can do everything through Christ, who gives me strength. (Phil. 4:11–13)

Some of us are buying up more than we need because we're discontent with the life that we have. More will never make you happier. Only God can fulfill the deep need that you're grappling with today.

As an extra bonus, Paul points out that a by-product of contentment is strength. We're stronger because life's shifting winds and changing circumstances can't blow us down. We're stronger when our happiness and peace are anchored in Christ.

Take a moment and consider what's around you or even what's in your favorite online shopping carts. It takes courage to admit that your retail therapy is a coping tool, but honesty can lead to freedom.

Do I need to let go of something but can't break my emotional attachment to it?

In Matthew 6, Jesus warns against storing up treasures on earth. He says, "Store your treasures in heaven, where moths and rust cannot destroy, and thieves do not break in and steal. Wherever your treasure is, there the desires of your heart will also be" (vv. 20–21). He knows that our hearts will be attached to whatever we love. Some of the things we treasure represent stories that are near and dear to us. Is it possible to hold on to a precious memory and let go of the physical item we associate with it when it isn't helping our life?

Holding on to a possession due to emotional attachment is a reality that almost all of us face. For a variety of reasons, letting go of certain possessions isn't as simple as some people would like you to believe. If you struggle to let go of possessions because of an emotional attachment, before we go any further, I want you to know that you are seen and supported. For some of us, those emotional attachments are the result of trauma or mental illness, and working with a compassionate and knowledgeable mental health provider is necessary. But even for those who do not need professional assistance, emotional attachment still needs to be addressed because the practice of simplicity will be at odds with the desire to hold on to everything that has meaning attached.

During my divorce years ago, I debated whether to keep my home or move out. After more than twenty-five years of marriage, I wanted to have something substantial and tangible as a symbol of my life that survived our family's sadness. That home was where I raised my babies. As I cleaned out the attic, sorting through loads of family photos and touchstones of my adult life, I went through more than a box of tissues. At the same time, I needed to count the cost of keeping a large historical home that was prone to major mechanical systems failures and needed constant updating. I weighed the cost against my reality as a self-employed woman in ministry, and it was more than financial. My frequent travel schedule and career as a writer meant having to make a significant number of decisions each day, like planning trip logistics or long hours spent thinking of the right words for an article or book. I debated if it was wise to set myself up for the inevitable surprise of pipes that could burst at the wrong time or old wood that would need to be replaced.

In the end, I made the decision to let go of my home and move. It was hard and humbling to release that tangible presence in my life, but I do love the simplicity of living in a smaller, more manageable space where there is a low risk of decision fatigue. I can change my mind at any time when I'm ready to buy a house, but for now I don't have the weight of those extra decisions.

That's my story. You have your own journey to living out this practice. Simplicity should be Spirit-led conviction, not a one-size-fits-all application.

As you can see from my story, the emotional component of simplicity cannot be ignored. Our emotional attachments to stuff can be strong, which is why this journey needs to be Spirit-led. Practicing simplicity doesn't require us to ignore our emotions; however, practicing simplicity does require those emotions to be subject to the authority of God's Holy Spirit within us.

Maybe you struggle to let go of certain clothes even though they no longer support your well-being. Or maybe you struggle to let go of family possessions even though keeping them won't bring your loved one back. Maintaining all these possessions is adding to your overwhelm. Perhaps God is inviting you into an opportunity to let go of possessions and extra decisions so that you can enjoy a less stressful and more healthy life.

Principles for Establishing a Practice of Simplicity

1. **Prioritize loving God and others.** Determine what is getting in the way of your relationship with God or spending quality time with others.

2. **Investigate discontentment.** If there is an area in which you feel longing or dissatisfaction—whether it is about where you live, the car you drive, the income you make, or another area—invite God into that part of your life to move your heart toward contentment.

3. **Define your simplicity.** What types of decisions are draining you each day? How could you reduce the number of decisions you have to make? If you made fewer decisions, how would that simplicity ease the overwhelm or stress in your life?

4. **Cap your collection.** Determine now how much of any one hobby or collection you will keep. Develop a system to donate or sell items as you acquire new pieces.

5. **Ask simplicity questions.**

   • Am I able to sufficiently address the other obligations in my life before I add this to my schedule or take on this responsibility?

   • Will this decision or purchase increase my energy or time to love others, or will it take away from my energy and time?

   • Am I buying this because I'm trying to please someone else, live up to a certain expectation, raise my self-esteem, or reduce my guilt?

   • Do I have to buy or say yes to this now, or could I postpone the decision and revisit it six months from now?

Practical Ideas to Move toward Simplicity

1. Create a capsule wardrobe that consists of five shirts, five pairs of pants, five layering pieces (e.g., sweaters, blazers, vests), five pairs of shoes, and five dresses. (You can also create a capsule wardrobe for your kids.)

2. Establish a maximum number of certain household items that tend to get out of control; for example, brands of cereal, haircare products, streaming subscriptions, televisions.

3. Agree on three brands of products your family will use. You can switch out those brands in a family meeting every six months or annually.

4. Create and alternate two weekly menus to simplify shopping and dinner choices.

5. Institute a one-year fast from purchasing things that you already have too much of; for example, body lotions, certain clothing items, supplies for crafting or other hobbies.

6. Before busy months like May and December, predetermine the number of parties or special events that you will attend.

7. Implement a "get one, give one" policy in your home. For every new item that is purchased, a similar item should be donated.

8. Once a month, eliminate or donate the number of items equaling the number of days in that month.

11

TAKING CARE OF YOU

SELF-CARE

Now may the God of peace make you holy in every way,
and may your whole spirit and soul and body be kept
blameless until our Lord Jesus Christ comes again.

1 Thessalonians 5:23

While out at a dinner with a friend, writer Christine Miserandino grabbed twelve spoons and used them to explain what it's like living with a chronic illness. She calls it the "spoon theory."[1] Each spoon equals a unit of energy that Christine uses throughout the day on basic living tasks. Normal tasks like making dinner might take three spoons, and working all day would take five spoons. Christine also explains that higher pain days demand more spoons than lower pain days. For example, on a high pain day, the steps involved in taking a shower might need four spoons but only three spoons on a lower pain day. Those spoons represent the constant tension between what she needs to do each day versus the energy that she has left. Christine told her friend that if she's out of spoons by the end of her workday, she may have to cancel plans to meet friends for dinner or clean up her house. Pushing past her limit means that Christine would have to borrow spoons from the next day. At a certain point, the physical and mental deficit would shut down her body.

Christine recognized that her physical condition impacted what she could do and influenced the decisions that she made each day. While you may not contend with a chronic illness like Christine, you know that when your body feels healthy (or healthy for your physical condition), you have the capacity to do more and handle life with more energy. On the flip side, when you're feeling stressed or depleted, you can sense your body's sluggishness.

Everything that you think and do requires some level of energy. Just like we believe that recovery after exhaustion is better than resting to prevent exhaustion, we tend to believe that we'll have the energy to do everything that we say yes to.

As we reflect on Christine's spoon theory and the takeaways for us, two realities stand out:

1. We are all limited in our daily energy.
2. During seasons of overwhelm, we use more spoons more quickly because high emotional energy wears us down faster.

This leads us into a controversial conversation about the spiritual practice of self-care. The practice of self-care is anchored in the knowledge that we are caretakers of the bodies that God has created for us. A few people might argue that taking care of ourselves isn't important, but the tension seems to mostly circle around the question of whether discussing self-care is selfish or spiritual. As a speaker and author who spends a lot of time online, I've noticed that Christian women have an awkward relationship with self-care because they aren't sure if what is healthy and what is holy agree together. In my humble opinion, they do.

If God created our bodies in His image, and if Jesus, who is God, came to earth and took on human flesh, then our bodies are precious to God. I suspect that quite a few of us do not see our bodies that way. We see tummy fluff, stretch marks, wrinkles, or sadness because our bodies have betrayed us or have been abused.

In 1 Corinthians, Paul is writing to a group of believers who were using their bodies as a free-for-all. He reminds them of an important truth that we need today as well:

Don't you realize that your body is the temple of the Holy Spirit, who lives in you and was given to you by God? You do not belong to yourself. (6:19)

Even though you may not like what you see in the mirror, God certainly doesn't view your body as a worthless, disposable takeout container. Yes, our bodies are imperfect, and they break down because they bear the consequences of sin and death. Yet God plans to redeem our skin and bones one day. When God created our human form, we carried His stamp of goodness and He plans to bring that goodness back. We see this foreshadowed at Jesus's resurrection from the dead, when the risen Lord appeared to His followers and showed them His glorified human body (Luke 24:39). We can look forward to the day when we, too, will inhabit our bodies in their eternal, glorified form (Phil. 3:20–21).

Some of us have developed a habit of treating our bodies like they don't matter. We use our bodies like workhorses, piling on weight without regard to the crushing load, running them ragged all day long. I'd argue that workhorses are treated much better than we treat ourselves, people made in the image of God. At the end of the day, a horse owner will brush down the horse and check its body for injuries before giving it good food and water. On the flip side, we drag our bodies to the couch, feeling our aches and pains, and eat another pint of ice cream instead of going to bed.

Depending on where you are on the continuum of self-care, the voices of condemnation may be singing a chorus at you right now about the mistakes that you've made, accusing you of being lazy or a failure. There is no condemnation for God's children—including you. The great news is that it's never too late to start or to start over. As with any other spiritual practice, when you make space for God to speak into and transform this area of your life, you'll discover the rhythms that are right for you. Each of us is unique and our bodies are different from one another, but we all can practice self-care the same as we all can engage in the other spiritual practices.

The spiritual practice of self-care recognizes that when we care for these bodies God created, that care is an act of worship to God. I love how my friend and fellow author Katy Mc-Cown often asks, "Am I taking care of myself for the sake of my Savior?"

There are lots of different options for how to approach self-care as a spiritual practice, but I'd like to cover four areas that we see reflected in biblical teaching and practice: sleep, exercise, nutrition, and clothing. These aren't the only self-care areas addressed in Scripture, but these specifically impact women who struggle with stress and overwhelm. As you reflect on the teaching of Scripture, hold on to the truth that your body is not your own. That skin you're in is owned by God. While there are no easy answers for why some bodies work better than others, we're all called to honor God with what He has given us.

Sleep

> It is useless for you to work so hard
> from early morning until late at night,
> anxiously working for food to eat;
> for God gives rest to his loved ones. (Ps. 127:2)

Sleep is one of the first casualties of our battle with overwhelm. When we're stressed, our bodies struggle to sleep. Whether anxiety is keeping us awake, possibly in fight-or-flight survival mode, or we keep working, thinking that we'll catch up or get ahead, we sacrifice our sleep without understanding the true impact it has on our bodies.

According to the National Institutes of Health, 50 to 70 million Americans suffer from chronic sleep disorders, which means that their lack of sleep is putting their health and lives at risk.[2] An increased risk of high blood pressure, obesity, heart attack, and stroke can be traced to sleep dysfunction. Health care professionals recommend seven hours of sleep per night; anything less is considered sleep loss.

Are you aware of how much sleep you are getting each night? The first step in knowing whether sleep is a problem for you is finding out how much sleep you're getting each night. During my difficult years, I purchased a fitness tracker that provided a daily report of how much sleep I'd get each night. It was helpful accountability for me to see the hard numbers so that I could be real with myself.

In seasons of high stress during our family's crisis, there was a lot in my life that I couldn't control, but I could discipline myself toward better sleep. Some helpful tools that I used during those long years included taking a nightly walk to dissipate some of the stress that had built up in my body throughout the day. I removed the television from my bedroom and plugged in my phone in my office to prevent technology from keeping me up. To battle anxious thoughts after I lay down, I kept a note card next to my bed with five promises of God written on it. When my mind would start spinning and my heart would race, I'd pull out that card and let God's Word reassure me.

While those tools are helpful, there's an aha moment that I want to share with you. First, look at the following Bible verses about sleep and consider them in the context of self-care:

> You can go to bed without fear;
> you will lie down and sleep soundly. (Prov. 3:24)

> Indeed, he who watches over Israel never slumbers or sleeps. (Ps. 121:4)

When I looked at verses specifically about the connection between sleep and our mental state, it occurred to me that our inability to sleep could be tied to our attempts to control. Whether we're staying up late to keep working or endlessly spinning our mental wheels looking for solutions, we're missing out on sleep because we're trying to solve problems or fix situations that might be better served surrendering to God. This was an aha moment for me because I'm a night person and it's easy for me to stay up and keep working. I'm the queen of "just one more thing," and before you know it, the clock reads 1:00 a.m. and I wanted to go to bed hours before.

Psalm 121:4 is an especially powerful reminder that God doesn't need sleep. He sends us to bed as a reminder that He can handle our world while we are sleeping.

Here are two practical tools to help quiet your mind as you prepare for sleep:

1. *Create a God Box.* If it's hard for you to settle down at night, one solution would be to create a God Box. There are examples of these all over the internet. You can decorate the box or keep it simple. Before bed or if you're

having trouble falling asleep, you write out your fears, concerns, or thoughts as prayers to God and put them in the box. As 1 Peter 5:7 says, "Give all your worries and cares to God, for he cares about you."

2. *Journal.* Like the God Box activity, this involves writing down whatever is on your mind before bed. In the journal, however, you're directed toward writing out gratitude lists, making to-do lists for things that are on your mind, or writing down two or three important things that happened during the day. The journal helps you calm down by reflecting and also clears your brain of any thoughts that might not be settled.

Exercise

It might surprise you to realize that you need to prepare your body to serve God and others.

When you say yes to Jesus, God has a great adventure of faith and purpose waiting for you. While it can take time to understand what specific assignments might look like, one thing is for sure: when we are serving God, we're often using more energy and moving our bodies in different ways from our regular rhythms of life. If you volunteer in the nursery, serve with the high school students, teach Bible study, or sing on the worship team, those activities involve a different kind of energy and often require a greater energy output. For example, if you've ever taught a Bible lesson to three-year-olds, that can tire you out quicker than sitting in front of your computer at work.

According to the world, the goal of exercise is to make our bodies look better, to be stronger, to impress others, and to stay healthy for our loved ones. However, when we think about exercise as part of a self-care practice, the goal is to equip our bodies for God to use us in ministry. Disciplining your body strengthens you for the demands of your God-given assignment.

Paul considered himself lucky to be given the gift of sharing the gospel, so he took care of his body in such a way that he could live out his calling. He often liked to use athletic imagery, so he compared his preparation as a missionary to an athlete preparing for a race:

> I discipline my body like an athlete, training it to do what it should. Otherwise, I fear that after preaching to others I myself might be disqualified. (1 Cor. 9:27)

While Paul doesn't go into detail about what types of physical training he did, for Paul to endure his adventures and misadventures, it makes sense that he'd engage in some form of physical training and pay attention to how he nourished his body and managed his stress. Not only that, but Paul also had to contend with his mysterious "thorn in my flesh" (2 Cor. 12:7), so that also had an impact on his overall physical and mental health.

None of us has a perfect body. Even if we're in good health, our bodies can still face injury, aging, or sudden illness. Yet, God can use us no matter what condition our bodies are in.

In 1967, Joni Eareckson Tada experienced a water accident that left her as a quadriplegic. For decades, Joni has shared her story of faith and overcoming and has served as an advocate for those suffering from physical challenges. She runs a large organization called Joni & Friends in addition to her partnerships with other organizations. In one of her radio shows, I heard Joni discuss her morning routine: "You see, I have this pretty standard morning routine: my girlfriend comes, exercises my legs, bathing, dressing, toileting, getting ready for the day, sitting up in the wheelchair. It's a routine I haven't altered in years."[3] Even with her limited physical abilities, notice what she includes. Joni incorporates exercise because it's a discipline that's good for her body, even though her body doesn't work as it should. Joni does what she can, and I hope her example encourages you to do what you can, when you can, and not give up!

Do you sense God speaking to you here? Perhaps a visit to your healthcare provider is needed. Maybe you will decide to take a walk each day and ask a friend to hold you accountable. I use a fitness tracker to provide honest feedback about how often I'm moving my body so that I can't lie to myself.

We all have different physical conditions. However, you can be strong at whatever level you are. One of the ways you can let God know that you're ready for whatever purpose He has for you is to consistently keep your body prepared. You never know where He'll want to send you, use you, or elevate you, but your responsibility is to be ready for it!

Nutrition

If the saying is true that you are what you eat, what have you been eating lately? Stress eating is a whole thing, and most all of us have been there. Once upon a time, I had a passionate relationship with Snickers bars. They were always there for me when work was wild or the laundry piled up. Food is a mood changer, so when we're stressed, eating something satisfying can be a fast way to feel better. But is that God's best for us?

On the flip side, food is an important way of showing love and support when people are coping with stress. When people are sick or lose a loved one, bringing over a dish or dropping off a freezer meal is a way of expressing love through food. So how do we balance it all?

Paul keeps it simple and nonjudgmental when it comes to making food decisions:

> So whether you eat or drink, or whatever you do, do it all for the glory of God. (1 Cor. 10:31)

Paul instructs believers to keep the goal in mind: God's glory. There's no approved Christian diet and there are no banned foods. Eat to glorify God. There's guidance and freedom in that! This means that our relationship with food should involve asking the Holy Spirit to guide us on what's best for us. Perhaps right now you can think of some foods that do not bless you when you eat them. You might joke about it, but you know your body doesn't respond well to them or the doctor has asked you to refrain. Could God's Spirit use your body's responses or your healthcare provider's input to help you discern how to honor Him? Yes, it's possible.

As someone with a long history of emotional eating, I've wrestled with the pull toward all things creamy and sweet when I'm stressed. Engaging with spiritual practices like sacrifice and submission have helped me focus on God over food. I've learned that we truly do not live by bread alone but only by the strength and power of God.

What if you were to take a day and before each meal, pray and ask God to give you input on what to eat or feedback after you eat? While God doesn't usually speak in an audible voice, He will answer your prayer if the goal is to honor Him with what you consume. You may sense a "yes" or "no" conviction when you scan the refrigerator. For me, there are certain junk foods that I lost interest in eating once I began focusing on healthier options. Invite the Holy Spirit into this area of your life and He will lead you.

Clothing

For years, I've been giving a talk titled "Taking Care of You: Becoming a Woman That CARES." It's based on 1 Peter 5:7, a verse I shared earlier in this chapter. This is a spiritual self-care talk that I've given all over the country to thousands of women. What's interesting is that Christian women are highly skeptical of this talk because it doesn't feel spiritual enough. I've overheard women wondering if the talk will have enough meat in it. I used to feel defensive, but now I just smile because I've seen how God works in unexpected places, like this topic that we're going to discuss as we wind down this chapter.

CARES is an acronym—because you know how much I love a good acronym. It stands for *clothing, appetite, rest, exercise,* and *smile.* What's also interesting is that when I finish the talk and women come up to me afterward, there's one area of the talk in which women feel most convicted by God: clothing. I can count on women lining up afterward to tell me, "Barb, as soon as I get home, I need to deal with my closet."

However, this self-care conversation is eternally bigger and more significant than motivation to toss out old clothes. Whether you realize this or not, how you feel about what you look like each day has a significant impact on whether you're open and willing to engage in gospel work and divine appointments.

Here's a verse that I share with ladies during the talk:

So we are Christ's ambassadors; God is making his appeal through us. We speak for Christ when we plead, "Come back to God!" (2 Cor. 5:20)

Think about it. When you finish dressing and you like the way you look—especially when you *really* like the way you look— that's often a day when you will look more people in the eye, be willing to have more conversations, and smile at people more often. These are all opportunities for a gospel impact.

On the flip side, if you put on your clothes and look in the mirror and frown, what are the chances that you'll put yourself out there for Jesus if an opportunity arises? I'm not saying that you won't, but I'd guess that you're more likely to do so on the days when you feel confident in how you look. It's hard to be Christ's ambassadors if we're feeling too badly about ourselves to get out into the world to talk about Jesus.

Do you need to turn this around? First, acknowledge that what you wear can influence how you feel about yourself and your willingness to connect with others. Second, ask yourself, "Do I have too many clothes?" If you think back to the practice of simplicity, how many extra decisions are you making each day because getting dressed in the morning is complicated? Some of you may need to weed through decades of old clothes mixed in with new ones. Or maybe you haven't purchased new clothes in decades, so you're trying to decide between old and outdated and older and even more outdated.

Here's what I can tell you on the other side of those closet struggles: if you can follow two practical steps, you can reduce the volume in your closet and simplify one of the hardest parts of a woman's day.

1. *Stop wearing clothes that make you sad.*

    You decide what sad looks like for you. As a rule, it's time to let go of any piece of clothing that makes you frown, causes you to feel frumpy, or lowers your self-esteem, no matter how much or how little you paid for the item. For some of you, this could be a lot of your wardrobe. That's okay. You won't be naked. Keeping sad clothes isn't taking care of yourself, and it can cause stress if wearing those clothes makes you feel uncomfortable, causes you to avoid people, or lowers your self-esteem.

2. *If it doesn't fit, get rid of it.*

    I know that you have certain favorites that you just want to hold on to. But keeping twelve different sizes in your closet is not healthy for you. Clothes that are too big are a source of fear because you never want to be that size again. But clothes that are too small mock or shame you because you haven't lost the weight to fit into them.

The blessing to you is knowing that every day when you dress, you'll feel ready to engage with the world instead of hoping that you can hide.

12

LETTING GOD LEAD

SUBMISSION

Take my yoke upon you. Let me teach you, because I am
humble and gentle at heart, and you will find rest for
your souls. For my yoke is easy to bear, and the burden
I give you is light.

Matthew 11:29–30

Let God lead. Those three words capture the big idea of submission as our next spiritual practice. Submission has become one of those embattled concepts in the Christian life, but it is a cornerstone practice because it demonstrates our willingness to allow God to reform our hearts, minds, and spirits to be more like Jesus.

Our flawed human interpretation of submission has been far removed from God's definition. Instead of being a life-giving spiritual practice that leads us to life and peace, submission has been demanded by spiritually perverted people to manipulate others. Submission has become a hammer when God designed it to be an invitation to holy blessing for His children.

For some of you, this spiritual practice will be challenging because you followed, trusted, and believed in spiritual leaders who did you wrong. If I can say this gently: God wasn't the one who did you wrong. We don't want to miss out on something good that God has for us because of some bad actors. If you've suffered because you submitted, I am a fellow sufferer with you. Growing up, I witnessed the confusion of seeing people who spoke for God but failed to act in ways that reflected the character or truth of God.

Our word *submission* is the joining of the prefix *sub-* and the word *mission*. The prefix *sub* means to come under, not in the sense of having inferior value but of getting into a proper order. The word *mission* relates to having a purpose or goal. So then, submission is the act of falling in line behind a purpose or goal. Submission is intended to be an act of free will, not force. Submission should also involve a worthy mission, not the whim of one seeking to grab power or intimidate.

Submitting to the Holy Spirit

The distinction between surrendering to God and submitting to God can be confusing. *Surrendering* is letting go of your way or your will, whereas *submitting* is saying yes to the gentle leading of God. Submission might not be a hot button for some people, but for people like me who have a strong fight impulse when stressed, this practice is a challenge.

I don't like people telling me what to do unless I've already decided it's something I want to do. Like a toddler who's learning about the world, it's easier for me to spit out "no" to a request than "yes," especially when it comes to the way of God.

When I'm stressed, my fight mode kicks in and my motto becomes "my way or the highway." Perhaps you lean more toward a freeze or fawn survival response and submission means that you may have to push out of your comfort zone.

One of the hallmarks of the Christian life is being led by the Spirit. And in Galatians 5, Paul talks about the natural progression of what happens when we are led by the Spirit versus when we allow our needs and desires to lead us. As you read the following verses, pay attention to the innate tension that we experience.

> So I say, let the Holy Spirit guide your lives. Then you won't be doing what your sinful nature craves. The sinful nature wants to do evil, which is just the opposite of what the Spirit wants. And the Spirit gives us desires that are the opposite of what the sinful nature desires. These two forces are constantly fighting each other, so you are not free to carry out your good intentions. (vv. 16–17)

The main reason Paul teaches us to let the Holy Spirit guide our lives is straightforward: we each have our own blind spots, and our refusal to admit that gets us into trouble. God also knew that we would confuse His lordship with the dazzling allure of other siren voices calling us to do what makes us feel good, to go get what we deserve.

Another observation that struck me is how the constant inner tension between wanting to do life our way versus God's way means that we will always have to deal with a baseline level of stress. Notice how Paul closes by saying that we're not free to carry out our good intentions. No matter how much willpower you wake up with every morning or how much you desire to live for Jesus, there will always be a conflict between what you want versus what God wants for you. It's possible for you to feel stress when you knowingly resist whatever God's

Spirit is prompting you to do. Years ago, I felt a strong tug to visit a neighbor in the hospital. I didn't like this neighbor, but I heard the whisper of the Holy Spirit telling me to go. I did not feel at peace until I was obedient and visited the neighbor. While I'm not sure of God's complete purpose, I was blessed by the visit and our neighborly relationship improved from that day forward.

The Gentle Leader

Our family's fourteen-year-old grandma dog, Quimby, is laying at my feet while I'm writing this. She has been the best dog that a family could ever have, and I will tell my future dogs exactly that. I believe God led us to her when she was a two-year-old dog in the animal shelter. Quimby sat and stared at us without making a sound while dogs all around us barked and pawed for attention. She had picked us, so we took her home. Quimby was glue in a broken family that was trying to put the pieces back together. Her glue was endless love, hope, and joy—except when it came to one thing: Quimby was a jerk every time we took her out for a walk.

Our sweet dog turned into an absolute maniac as soon as we snapped on her leash and stepped out the front door. After a few weeks of us getting pulled in all directions and suffering hyper-extended elbows, Dr. Google recommended a solution called the "Gentle Leader." Deceptively simple, the Gentle Leader was not a muzzle but a loop of half-inch nylon that went over Quimby's nose with two attached straps that would snap on top of her head. It was simple but highly effective. Whenever Quimby pulled on her leash, the tension would transfer from the Gentle Leader and tug her nose to the side. Since dogs can't walk with their nose turned to the side, Quimby would immediately stop walking and therefore stop pulling. Problem solved. I appreciated the Gentle Leader because we were able to correct a troublesome, difficult, and at times painful behavior in a way that didn't require any harsh punishment or shock.

Fast-forward to the present. You'd think that after more than a decade of wearing a Gentle Leader, Quimby would no longer need it. After all this time, she should know better and not pull her leash to check out that little squirrel or sniff every single bush, right? Nope. Bless that sweet dog's wandering heart, she lives to pull, even though her pace is slower now.

But a very interesting thing happened after the first few years. Initially, Quimby would fight us whenever we pulled out the Gentle Leader and tried to put it on her. Now, however, Quimby comes over, sits down, and slips her nose through the nylon loop. While her zest for sniffing trees, checking out every single bush, or just going off on her own has never changed, she has adjusted to letting us lead her along the way.

We have a Gentle Leader in God's Holy Spirit. Successfully practicing submission begins with realizing our need to be led every day and never getting to the point where we think that we don't need God's leading or correction. There are times on our path when we pull, and the Holy Spirit gets our attention by stopping us from charging ahead. This is not a punishment; rather, it is a kind and gracious act of God. He offers gentle nudges intended to get us to pause, reflect, slow down, and align ourselves with Him again.

Being led by the Spirit doesn't mean that you turn into a robot. Practicing submission is a choice and a freedom. It's a choice because God isn't making you do anything. You choose whether you want to submit to His leading.

One afternoon while I was on a trip to Savannah, I left my hotel to hustle on foot toward downtown to visit a historic church before leaving town. I turned on my GPS and headed in the direction of the church, hoping to make it in time for the final tour of their Underground Railroad exhibit. As I fast-walked down a side street, I noticed a young man coming toward me with his head down. The streets weren't overly crowded, but there were a lot of people out walking. Yet, there was something about this young man that caught my attention. I felt a nudge from the Holy Spirit whisper, "Tell him that God loves him."

I had sunglasses on, so no one could see my eyes widen as that whisper registered in my mind. My response was quick: "God, You want me to stop and talk to a perfect stranger in a strange town. He's going to think I'm weird."

The young man continued to approach, and I kept up my pace. I didn't want to be disobedient, but I also didn't want to look stupid.

As the young man passed by me in a crosswalk, my heart sank because I'd failed to do what I sensed God clearly asking me to do. A few moments later, while I was still in the crosswalk, I whirled around and projected my voice: "Excuse me."

Nothing. He kept walking. I spoke louder: "EXCUSE ME."

The young man turned and looked at me.

I fumbled my words for a moment, which is unusual considering what I do. But I finally got myself together and spoke. "This might sound strange, but God wanted me to tell you that He loves you."

This time, the young man's eyes widened and he tilted his head.

I shuffled my feet and looked down. It was a hot day, but my face heated even more from bashful embarrassment.

He spoke up. "Wow. That's wild. I'm having a really bad day. I needed to hear that today."

He didn't smile, but I could see that just a little heaviness around him had lifted. He turned and continued on his way.

I have no idea why God chose me to speak to that young man on that particular day. Submitting to the Spirit's leading sometimes means that I don't know, but I can trust that God is good and is doing something good. For me, the blessing came from joining God in His kingdom plan even though I have no idea what His plan is for that young man's life. I'm satisfied and blessed knowing that I did my part.

What about you? Submitting to God's Holy Spirit isn't easy, especially if you sense God calling you to take hard steps like offering forgiveness, turning away from certain desires, or trusting Him without being able to see the path ahead. Yet, Paul prays for believers to fully trust in God and let His Spirit lead so that we will experience abundance and overflow in our lives rather than overwhelm. Here's what he prays for us:

> I pray that God, the source of hope, will fill you completely with joy and peace because you trust in him. Then you will overflow with confident hope through the power of the Holy Spirit. (Rom. 15:13)

Here are a few prayer prompts for inviting the Holy Spirit to speak to you as part of practicing submission:

1. God, examine my heart and open my eyes to any area in my life where I am afraid or unwilling to wholly trust You.
2. God, is there a step of obedience that I haven't taken that You've been waiting on me to take?
3. God, is there a habit or pattern of behavior that is unhealthy for me physically that I need to submit to You?
4. God, I give You permission to lead me today. I want to follow Your plan and purpose for my life today.

13

GIVING UP FOR GOD'S HOLY GOOD

SACRIFICE

Keep a space where God can let something totally new
take place.

Henri Nouwen

When was the last time that you gave up something you love
for something you love more?

Most parents understand the concept of sacrifice. It's not
what they give up that matters but *why* they are giving it up.
When I was fifteen years old, my working-class parents paid
hundreds of dollars for me to wear contacts because I'd been
made fun of since childhood for my pop-bottle-thick glasses.
A lifetime of years later, I don't know what my parents gave
up, figured out, or shuffled around to afford such an opportunity for me. For sure, that money wasn't just lying around.

All I know is why they made those sacrifices: *love*. Once I became a parent, it all made sense. Sacrifice is one of the most powerful expressions of love or commitment that we can offer to others.

In our country, we're grateful for our armed services. The freedom that we enjoy today is because of the generations of soldiers who have sacrificed their lives for our freedom. As the mother of an Army officer, the knowledge that my child has made the decision to put their life on the line for our country terrifies me and fills me with pride all at the same time.

Exploring the spiritual practice of sacrifice might be a challenging topic to explore if you feel like you're already making too many sacrifices. Some of those sacrifices might feel like they are at the expense of your emotional, financial, and mental health. Perhaps one or more of the following sacrifices feel familiar:

- Sacrificing sleep to work a side business to build financial security.
- Giving up haircuts or buying clothes to pay for your kids' extracurriculars.
- Skimming money off your slim budget to help your college student or aging parents.
- Postponing or setting aside your dreams to give someone else in your life the opportunity to pursue theirs.

Sacrifice is admirable, but when we make too many sacrifices for too long, the stress of undermining our mental or emotional security can overwhelm us. God does not call us to sacrifice in a way that makes it difficult for us to live out kingdom priorities.

The spiritual practice of sacrifice is about giving up for God's holy good. However, God never demands that we sacrifice in an unhealthy way.

Sacrifice is an extension of surrender. With surrender, we give over what we can't control and let go of the outcome. With sacrifice, we give up what makes us feel secure or satisfied for something more valuable or important. Sacrifice is sometimes the first step in surrender, but that doesn't mean surrender is always a part of sacrifice.

Why is sacrifice a valuable spiritual practice for us? B. B. Warfield writes, "In a very real sense it [the theme of sacrifice] constitutes Christianity. It is this which differentiates Christianity from other religions. . . . It came to proclaim the real sacrifice for sin which God had provided in order to supersede all the poor fumbling efforts which men made and were making to provide a sacrifice for sin for themselves."[1]

Sacrificing to See God's Mighty Power at Work

When it comes to sacrifice, our human history is messy, especially when you look in the Bible. Once humans sinned, animals had to be sacrificed as part of the penalty of sin. The first sacrifice occurred in the garden of Eden when God slaughtered an animal to make clothes for Adam and Eve after they sinned (Gen. 3:21). Later, Cain and Abel made sacrifices, but Cain murdered his brother after God rejected Cain's sacrifice (Gen. 4).

Then there's the tragic story of Jephthah, a judge in Israel, who vowed to sacrifice the first thing that came out his door if God gave him victory in battle. When he returned home after winning, his daughter came out to meet him (Judg. 11:30–39). Scholars debate whether Jephthah went through with the sacrifice, but verse 39 seems to indicate that he did what he said he would do.

One of the most difficult stories in the Bible for me is found in Genesis 22, when God tested Abraham's faith by asking him to sacrifice his son Isaac:

Take your son, your only son—yes, Isaac, whom you love so much—and go to the land of Moriah. Go and sacrifice him as a burnt offering on one of the mountains, which I will show you. (v. 2)

After a lifetime of infertility, missteps, and waiting, Abraham and his wife, Sarah, had finally received their promised son, Isaac. While they had some family drama where they mistreated their servant Hagar and Ishmael, Abraham's son with Hagar, it's not hard to imagine the joy of holding a much-loved and long-awaited child. So Abraham must have been puzzled by what God was asking him to do.

In the ancient Near East, child sacrifices by pagan nations were abominable but common, so Abraham may not have been too surprised. Abraham may have wondered why God would promise that he'd have more descendants than stars in the sky if his son of promise was about to die before having children (Gen. 15:4–5; 21:12). Later, in Hebrews 11:17–19, we are told that Abraham obeyed God because he believed that God could raise Isaac from the dead.

Still, Abraham woke up the next morning and left early. He didn't stall or try to bargain with God. He got up, prepared to follow God's instruction, and left home with Isaac and two servants. Of course, as a mother, I've always wondered what he told Sarah and how that whole conversation went down the night before.

When Abraham, Isaac, and the servants arrived at Mount Moriah, Abraham took Isaac and just the two of them went up the mountain together. Think about what must have been going through Abraham's mind. What must have been going through Isaac's mind as his father tied him up and laid him across the top of the wood? Isaac had known they would be making a sacrifice, but not until that point would Isaac have realized that *he* was the sacrifice.

The reason I have struggled with this story is that I wonder how God could ask Abraham to give up what he loved. The Bible says it was to test Abraham's faith in God, and God commends Abraham for his faith and again affirms His promise for a long line of descendants.

For me, the significance of this story is in the way it foreshadows the magnitude of God's love for us. After God sent an angel to stop Abraham from sacrificing Isaac, Abraham looked up and saw a ram caught in a thicket, and he sacrificed the ram as a substitute. It's a beautiful foreshadowing of how, out of His great love for us, God allowed His only Son to be sacrificed on our behalf.

As believers, we are to imitate Christ. While our daily discipleship may not require physically sacrificing ourselves for others, the practice of sacrifice calls us to lay down our lives to live out the gospel.

In his letter to the Philippians, Paul declares his intention to live a sacrificial life:

> I want to know Christ and experience the mighty power that raised him from the dead. I want to suffer with him, sharing in his death. (3:10)

Paul could have remained a tentmaker in Tarsus. While there were no guarantees that he would live an easy life, Paul would not have encountered harrowing, stressful situations like dangerous journeys between continents, opposition from Jewish leaders, shipwrecks, death threats, and hunger. He sacrificed what could have been a predictable life for a significant life.

In his letter to the Romans, Paul gives a picture of what this looks like in practice:

> And so, dear brothers and sisters, I plead with you to give your bodies to God because of all he has done for you. Let them be a

living and holy sacrifice—the kind he will find acceptable. This is truly the way to worship him. (12:1)

Paul calls believers to give their bodies to God as "living and holy" sacrifices just as Jesus was our living sacrifice.

How do we cooperate with the Spirit's work in us? Here are a few practical examples of how you could exercise the spiritual practice of sacrifice:

- Fasting from food, electronics, shopping, or social media
- Practicing financial generosity, including tithing
- Letting go of a relationship that doesn't honor God
- Switching careers to increase available time for kingdom priorities

I've been blessed to witness many examples of Spirit-led sacrifice. After months of prayer, a friend and her husband took a high school student into their home for several months when the student's parents were unable to take care of them. This was a sacrifice because my friends assumed financial responsibility for the student's care as well as responsibility for nurturing and guiding the student through the emotional turmoil.

Another friend and her husband have been married for over twenty years. When they married, they looked forward to a life in ministry together. Both are talented leaders, but when her husband was offered a senior leadership position, my friend knew that God was calling her to balance his new role by modifying her leadership so that she could offer extra support at home.

Yet another friend and her husband paid off their home years ago. While they could afford a much larger and more luxurious home, they've chosen to remain in their home so that they can be flexible for whatever and wherever God leads.

These are all examples of Holy Spirit–led sacrifice that looks different for everyone.

Fasting as a Spiritual Tool to Practice Sacrifice

In this next section, we'll look at another type of sacrifice that is a powerful training tool, especially if you recognize that you need to develop more self-control and dependence on God in your life.

Fasting is a personal discipline of sacrifice between you and God. This is a common form of sacrifice where you choose to give up something that you value for something more important. Most of us associate fasting with food, which is necessary for our survival. Food also serves other important needs in our lives. We use food to connect with others and to soothe ourselves. We don't call it comfort food for nothing!

In the Bible, there are numerous examples of people fasting for various reasons:

> Moses remained there on the mountain with the LORD forty days and forty nights. In all that time he ate no bread and drank no water. (Exod. 34:28)

> Jehoshaphat was terrified by this news and begged the Lord for guidance. He also ordered everyone in Judah to begin fasting. (2 Chron. 20:3)

> As news of the king's decree reached all the provinces, there was great mourning among the Jews. They fasted, wept, and wailed, and many people lay in burlap and ashes. (Esther 4:3)

When Jesus taught about fasting, He didn't present it as an optional activity.

> And *when you fast*, don't make it obvious, as the hypocrites do, for they try to look miserable and disheveled so people will

admire them for their fasting. I tell you the truth, that is the only reward they will ever get. (Matt. 6:16)

Jesus says "when you fast" to indicate that at some point this form of sacrifice will be part of a believer's life. Jesus also taught about the proper attitude around fasting, which is different from the public show of piety that the Jewish religious leaders put on to impress others.

Fasting can be practiced on your own or with others. For example, my church participates in a collective fast each year; having community support can be an encouragement to keep going. Jesus also fasted while He was alone in the wilderness as His final preparation before public ministry. One of the most important statements that Jesus shared during that time came after Satan tempted Him to turn rocks into loaves of bread. Jesus rebuked the devil by quoting from Deuteronomy 8:3:

But Jesus told him, "No! The Scriptures say, 'People do not live by bread alone, but by every word that comes from the mouth of God.'" (Matt. 4:4)

As much as I considered my faith to be the most important part of my life, I resisted any type of fasting from food. While there are religions like Islam that normalize regular seasons of fasting, it was not a topic that came up in my Black Baptist church. Now, as an adult reflecting on why fasting was never discussed, I wonder if it was because the difficulties of racism and prejudice made people feel like enough had been sacrificed already, so giving up a main source of community comfort was too much.

I carried that reluctance to fast through my twenties and thirties, even though I belonged to a church and worked on staff. When I read Richard Foster's *Celebration of Discipline* for the first time, there was a shift in my emotional universe when

I read these words in his chapter on fasting: "More than any other Discipline, fasting reveals the things that control us." He goes on to say, "We cover up what is inside us with food and other good things, but in fasting these things surface."[2] Fasting is like a truth serum that shakes us out of denial about what's really happening inside of us.

During those years, I knew that emotional eating was a habit for me. At the time, there was no external evidence that this habit was a problem, but I had a niggling feeling inside that food had a stronger hold on me than it should have. As an unrepentant workaholic during those years, I'd dream of what to eat for dinner as a way of relieving stress while I was at work. I had special meals that I'd make for myself as rewards whenever I was having a bad day.

After reading Foster's quote, I instantly sensed God's conviction in this area. If you've ever done a fast, you might have had the feeling within the first six hours that you would die from not eating. At first, I'd experience a little weakness, and my body made me feel like I was betraying it. But I didn't die. Based on my body's rebellion, I knew that God wanted me to submit to this spiritual practice.

About a decade ago, I woke up one morning with the conviction from God to fast once a week. I didn't hear God in an audible voice, but I knew that it was Him. Two months earlier, I'd had a clear sign that a significant spiritual battle was coming. I needed the practice of fasting as a means of increasing my limited self-control and learning how to live by the leading of the Spirit. I knew that if I didn't learn to fast, I would emotionally eat through our family crisis and create more problems for myself.

I began my weekly fast the next day, which coincided with a new season of spiritual challenge that began that same day. As much as I longed to not fast, it seemed God confirmed that I needed to do it as part of my battle against overwhelm. I prayed over how to do the fast and settled on a liquid-only fast from Tuesday night through Thursday morning each week. In those early months, my fasting days intensified the stress that I was feeling at work and home. I'd dream of brownies or ice cream or other favorite go-to stress foods. It seemed like this spiritual practice had the opposite effect from bringing peace.

But I didn't quit. I wanted to, yet I also knew God wanted to do something for me and in me, and fasting was the tool that He used. I love how Mahesh Chavda describes fasting: "We don't fast to earn something; we fast to make a connection with our supernatural God. We are cleaning out the 'pipe' that connects us to the anointing of God."[3]

My physical hunger put pressure on the weak areas that I hadn't taken seriously as a threat to my faith. Fasting forced the flimsy veneers around my inner thoughts and attitudes to collapse. I was surprised at some of the unkind thoughts, obsessions, and rebellion that surfaced in my spirit. During my fast, I could repent from those thoughts and obsessions. As Jesus taught in Matthew 4:4, I fed my spirit with Scripture, prayer, and meditation. It was humbling but also freeing when I could let God into those messy areas of my life.

God used fasting to make me strong. While fasting never comes easy, I've grown in strength to handle it, and that strength has blessed me in other areas. Learning how to delay gratification and increase my dependence on God has helped me avoid seeking out stress-relievers that would backfire on me such as overspending, overeating, and impatience. As stressors have come, fasting has trained me to not only know but also experience God's faithfulness and to seek comfort in Him instead of in other ways.

If you don't like the feeling of getting knocked over every time something spiritually difficult comes your way, fasting trains you for adversity. Years ago, I gave a keynote message at a leadership event and stayed to hear the afternoon speaker. He was at that time the CEO of an endurance race organization, and in his talk "Training for Adversity," he shared about his morning routine of doing three hundred burpees and taking a cold shower.[4] First thing every day, he accomplished two difficult things to increase his capacity to do more difficult things through the rest of his day. My takeaway was that God helps us practice hard things when it is easier so that we can do the hard things when we don't want to.

I still practice my weekly fast. Each year at the end of June, I pray and wait for a leading from God about whether I should continue that practice. Maybe one day I'll sense that I don't need to anymore, but that hasn't happened yet. It's still a challenge each week, but I am convinced that this practice allows me to experience a deeper connection with God and builds in me a spiritual confidence that is based on the deepening strength I receive from God rather than my reliance upon myself.

Take a Next Step: Begin Your Fasting Practice

Now it's your turn. Here is a practical guide to begin a fast as part of practicing sacrifice. There are many ways to do a fast, but this is a flexible framework that you can adapt as you need to.

1. Pray and invite God into this new adventure of faith. Ask Him to give you clarity about what type of fasting would be beneficial for you.
2. Pick a window of fasting, whether it's a single meal to start or a whole day.
3. Discern the purpose of your fast. Here are some questions that you can pray and journal about:
   • What possession distracts or influences you more than it should?

- What behavior or habit is creating conflict with the people in your life?
- Where do you overindulge in a way that you know isn't healthy?
- In what areas do you need to develop more patience?
- What do you sense God calling you to let go of?

4. Choose the type of fast that you will do. Food? Electronics? Clothes shopping? A certain activity such as alcohol consumption or a type of entertainment?
5. Either ask a friend to fast with you for support or ask a friend to pray for you on your fast day.
6. On the day of the fast, use the time when you'd normally engage in that activity to instead pray or listen to worship music.

A few reminders: You may feel overwhelmed at the thought of an entire day of fasting, but focus on one hour at a time. Remind your mind and body that God will sustain you through whatever you've sacrificed. Finally, fasting isn't a pass/fail grade on your faith. If you end the fast sooner than planned, don't fall into the trap of thinking that God is disappointed in you. Let it go. Try it again.

Jesus taught that fasting should be a regular part of a believer's life, and this practice plays a vital role in creating space for God to strengthen you in a unique way that is different from any other practice. I can tell you from a decade of personal experience that a regular practice of giving up something you love for something you love more allows God room to cement your inner core with a strength and peace in Him that will bless you in untold ways.

14

LEAN ON ME

SISTERHOOD

When you and I choose to enter into these sacred spaces, sharing our scars while honoring another's, something otherworldly happens. Something holy.

Michele Cushatt

Over my years as a ministry leader, life coach, and speaker, I've had countless women from around the country write or whisper to me, "I really don't trust women" or "It's hard to find a good friend." Even though they may subscribe to my weekly Happy Monday devotional or attend a women's event, large numbers of women who reach out to me are living in a barren vacuum without significant connection to other women who share their faith in Christ. If that's you, I know that your heart is aching. My heart aches for you too.

We all want connection. We long to be known by others. In her book *Daring Greatly*, researcher Brené Brown studies the importance of connection and writes, "Connection is why we're here. We are hardwired to connect with others, it's what gives purpose and meaning to our lives, and without it there is suffering."[1]

When people believe that they are abandoned or all alone, this pierces the heart of God. As we're navigating a swirling vortex of constant social and technological change, far too many people report feeling left out and alone.

The alarm has been sounded. In May 2023, the surgeon general launched a national campaign to combat what he declared our nation's next great health crisis. "Loneliness raises risk of heart disease and dementia, some research reporting the danger of loneliness as more lethal than smoking almost 15 cigarettes per day."[2]

The spiritual practice of sisterhood is your commitment to using your connection to Christ to create strong bonds with other sisters in Christ. Yes, the body of Christ is made of women and men who love Jesus, but sisterhood fulfills a specific need in the life of an overwhelmed woman. With one, two, or a group of other women, a stressed or overwhelmed woman knows that there are women who have her back and remind her that God does too.

Long ago, the writer of Ecclesiastes pointed out that lone-ranger living is less than desirable:

> Two people are better off than one, for they can help each other succeed. If one person falls, the other can reach out and help. But someone who falls alone is in real trouble. Likewise, two people lying close together can keep each other warm. But how can one be warm alone? A person standing alone can be attacked and defeated. (4:9–12)

When life is stressful, the worst thing that we can do is run away and not allow others to help us. Our fear of shame, embarrassment, or consequences is real, but it isn't the only reality. When you run, your problems chase you. Not only that, but other chasing beasts like depression, discouragement, and suicidal thoughts close in for the spiritual attack. You need help or else they will defeat you.

As I adjusted to life as a single person again, I battled through the grief of my loss and the shame that comes with divorce, even though it wasn't my choice. For a time, church was a struggle because of all the couples I saw and the memories of when I used to attend church with my former spouse. The magnetic pull toward hunkering down and keeping to myself was strong. I thought about how our ancient enemy zeroes in on our weakness and isolation to drown us with lies because we wouldn't have anyone around to help us.

As I thought about Ecclesiastes 4, I reached out to my friend Marguerite. We'd known each other for more than a decade but began talking more when she joined the test group for my *Surrendered* Bible study. Sadly, we both experienced the death of our longtime marriages around the same time. We decided to colead a divorce care group together. When we decided to reenter the dating world, I reached out to Marguerite to ask if we could meet once a month to talk and pray. I couldn't begin that new season of life without having someone to talk to who understood what I was going through. Over that first year, we would meet on a video call or in person at our favorite ice cream place. In promising to be completely honest with each other, we experienced freedom in knowing that another person was standing with and praying for us as we encountered the new terrain of our lives. I didn't feel vulnerable to Satan's lies, and I had support in the struggle.

Ecclesiastes 4:12 describes this kind of support:

Two can stand back-to-back and conquer. Three are even better, for a triple-braided cord is not easily broken.

Have you ever seen a photo or video of female elephants protecting a pregnant elephant in labor? The whole herd will surround the laboring mama and protect her from predators that could attack her in such a vulnerable state. The herd stomps its collective feet and kicks up dirt at any animal that tries to advance on the mama. They show up for her. They surround her to protect her. This is the kind of sisterhood that Christian women need to be for one another in an overwhelming world.

The Humility of Admitting Our Need

How good are you at receiving from others?

Even as our country experiences a crisis of loneliness, the good news is that God has already addressed that problem with both earthly and eternal solutions. As we look at the godly spiritual practice of sisterhood as a type of Christian community, our focus will be on how nurturing relationships with other Christian women is exactly what we need to be supported well in stressful times. Growing in this spiritual practice also gives us an opportunity to experience a taste of what it means to be part of God's family, loved, cared for, and provided for in every situation.

What God has designed for us is what the world is missing right now: connection. And it's not just the world that's missing it; Christians are missing it too.

What happened to our connections with others? We're spending less time in community and friendships. The surgeon general's report on loneliness notes that between 2003 and 2020, people spent sixty minutes per day with friends, but since 2020, people spend only twenty minutes per day with friends. While it's true that there are more opportunities for online connections, experts agree that in-person connections are richer, deeper, and more beneficial to our well-being. Experts point out that social media leads us to believe that we're more connected than we really are.

It's possible for us to be around other people and even to interact with them without experiencing connection. That's why this practice of sisterhood is so important. You will experience life-transforming change once you develop godly friendships with other godly women. You'll experience a sense of support, acceptance, and grace. When you live out this practice with others who do the same, you'll have a sisterhood of friends where you can come with your mask off and be real about your sins and struggles. This type of community is where healing happens. This is where we can confess the deepest, darkest parts of our lives in a safe place. Then we watch as the strongholds of fear, shame, and guilt break down like crumbling walls and we walk into a new journey of freedom.

In community, especially a sisterhood community, we can find wholeness and put our lives back together again. But it takes courage for us to do this. Not everyone has that courage at first.

Do You Need to Relax Your Quills?

Porcupines have never had their day in the sun as popular pets. Their faces are adorable, but they've got about 30,000 reasons why there are no viral videos documenting their cuddly cuteness. Their quills are no joke. Porcupines are covered in tens of thousands of quills to keep them safe when they feel threatened. For an animal or human unlucky enough to get quilled, those sharp spikes cause great pain when removed. A porcupine's basic message is "stay away from me." It's best not to argue with them.

Some of us have gotten used to putting out that same vibe. Unfortunately, our quills aren't as invisible as we think, and they have consequences. We grow an invisible quill each time someone gossips about us, lies to us, betrays us, abandons us, abuses us, diminishes us, or ignores us. We put up the quills because we have been hurt and we don't know how or where to find safe places to stop the hurt. Just for kicks, if you were a porcupine, how many quills would you have?

Some women are loud about their quills, and then there are the quiet quills of the woman who will give her name and maybe one or two details about her life. When you ask her how she's doing, she's going to respond with "I'm good" or "I'm fine" every single time. She's not giving up any more than that, and if you push her, she'll likely cut off contact.

Perhaps you've struggled to trust Christian women because they don't seem any different from the other adult mean girls that you encounter at work or in your friendships. We've all been there. But isolation isn't the answer. In our effort to protect ourselves from future pain, we hurt ourselves more by avoiding connection. To be clear, the hurt is real, but healing can only happen in safe Christian community with other believers surrounding us.

Jesus's half brother James wasn't originally one of Jesus's followers. There are hints in the Gospels that he wasn't on board with Jesus's earthly ministry, but Paul records that after the resurrection, Jesus appeared to James (1 Cor. 15:7), who then believed and became a powerful leader in the early church. Perhaps seeing Jesus's resurrected body was the evidence that James needed to become a believer.

In the New Testament letter that bears his name, James offers divine insight into how God uses other believers to help us when the brokenness of our world breaks us:

> Confess your sins to each other and pray for each other so that you may be healed. The earnest prayer of a righteous person has great power and produces wonderful results. (5:16)

While James teaches that healing is found in community, he doesn't give a timeline. Healing does take time. It's not always easy. But if we keep showing up for each other, we give healing a chance to happen.

It takes bravery and courage to practice community. There's no guarantee that other Christians won't hurt, betray, or abandon us. Jesus and Paul both experienced this, which sadly means that we will too. But community is a gamble that is worth the risk. Life is unpredictable, but community is one of the blessings that God gives us when life takes an unexpected turn.

Why Sisterhood Matters

My friend Laura had spent a beautiful day on the beach in Hilton Head with her thirteen-year-old daughter and a group of nine other teenage girls and three other moms. Just as they were about to settle down for bed back at their Airbnb in Savannah, Georgia, Laura's phone rang. She heard the scared voice of her twelve-year-old son back in Ohio. Within moments and with few details, Laura and her daughter were in the car driving back home with another mom. Laura's beloved husband, Jim, had taken his life by suicide in their backyard.

Within a few days of Jim's passing, Laura was faced with the unexpected challenge of figuring out what to do about a restaurant Jim had recently purchased as an investment in their small town. A successful architect, Jim had planned to update the restaurant before leasing it to a new operator.

Even as profound grief and all types of stress swirled, Laura seized an immediate opportunity. Before the funeral, she decided that the best place to hold the funeral luncheon would be at the restaurant. Laura told a friend that she'd need help getting the place cleaned out. All the equipment from the kitchen had been moved into the restaurant dining room. It was a tall order to get all the stuff moved and the place ready in time.

Within a few hours, dozens of us received a text message asking for help with cleaning and some heavy lifting. I was out of town visiting my oldest child, but I witnessed the text messages of support and photos that the women took with each other while cleaning.

Laura's friends rallied. They cleaned the restaurant in record time, and it was the perfect tribute to Jim to gather there with family and friends. But they didn't stop there. For months after Jim's death, Laura was showered with love in the form of meals, paper products so she wouldn't have to do dishes, notes of encouragement, gift cards for practical needs, yard work, and more.

Why did these women show up in such a powerful way? This is the power of sisterhood. When I think of sisterhood as a spiritual practice to support others, Laura's face comes to mind. As a longtime leader of our church's support group for moms, Laura had led by example in that large community of hundreds of moms. She organized countless meal trains, rallied moms together, organized mission trips, and offered her strong and steady presence where needed. In the days following Jim's passing, that large group of women rallied around Laura because years of love and connection drew them together when the stresses of life threatened to tear apart one of their own.

I also experienced Laura's sisterhood. At the end of my divorce years ago, Laura texted me because she and Jim wanted to offer me a complimentary stay in their lovely Airbnb on the water. She knew that I'd been overwhelmed, and she wanted to offer me support so that I could get away for a few days and rest before embarking on the new journey of putting my broken life back together.

Practicing Sisterhood and Making It Safe for All

If we're going to practice sisterhood as a godly spiritual practice, it's essential that we understand what makes it safe or unsafe, otherwise we'll pop up our quills and go it alone. Here are four principles that create safety so that you can practice sisterhood with others and experience the power and blessing of community—and connection.

We Are Better Together—But We Have to Actually Get Together

Make a commitment to each other to show up on a regular basis and not cancel when life gets difficult or inconvenient. Sisterhood can be in person or online—just make sure that it happens!

For the past seven years, I've met with my friend Cindy every other Wednesday. We meet at a local restaurant for one hour to talk about our faith, our lives, and God's leadings. We pray for each other and love to bring each other new snacks that we find at the store. While I travel a lot and she's got a busy job, Cindy and I don't cancel on each other unless one of us is sick or out of town. The blessing is knowing we can count on each other and will be there for each other in tough times.

More Listening and Learning, Less Lecturing

With the Bible at our fingertips, it's tempting to barrage someone with Bible verses in response to their sharing. There's nothing wrong with quoting Bible verses, especially since the Bible is the Word of God, but we need to consider our timing. Even though the person has opened up, we might not fully understand the situation. Spouting off a Bible verse without knowing the whole story can hurt instead of help.

The alternative is to put our energy into listening and learning from a sister who is stressed or overwhelmed. Asking good questions such as, "What's hard about this for you?" and "What are you praying about these days?" sends the message that she's cared for and also gives us greater insight into her situation.

Having insight opens the door for us to speak with wisdom if she requests our counsel.

Prayer

You know what comes to mind here? Female elephant stomping! Remember how those female elephants surrounded the laboring mama, stomping and kicking up dust to ward off threats? I feel like that's what we can do in prayer for each other. There are times when a woman will face a crisis or spiritual opposition, and beautiful, powerful sisterhood is surrounding her, supporting her, and fighting in prayer for her.

When you practice sisterhood, you let women show up and surround you, stomping it out in prayer against the enemy. And you do the same for them. Prayer is sweet and it is strong, and you have the privilege of offering that powerful combo!

Keep Confidence

There's a play on words here. First, we want to agree to the principle that whatever is said stays between those who are in the sisterhood unless someone is in danger of hurting themselves or others. Confidentiality should be a given, but it's always a good policy to remind each other that your conversations are sealed. It's so easy to let a minor detail or two slip when talking with others. But if you want a safe sisterhood community, complete confidentiality is the key. On the dedication page of this book, I mention the girlfriends who have been my sisterhood for many years, and God has used each of them in pivotal moments of my life.

The other side of this principle is to keep thinking the best of each other. It's no secret that women struggle in relationships with one another. Some of the difficulty happens when we begin to question a person's motives or character. God unconditionally loves us and calls us to love others unconditionally.

Practical Ways to Begin Your Sisterhood Practice

If you've never experienced sisterhood or you've had difficulty maintaining those relationships, I'm so proud that you've embraced reading this chapter. I am praying for you right now and trusting that God desires for you to experience rich, life-giving relationships with other Christian women. Here are some next steps for you to consider.

1. *Pray.* Tell God the desire of your heart, but be open to who God sends to you. Open yourself up to God's leading instead of looking for God to connect you with the most well-known or popular woman at church or in your group.

2. *Start with coffee questions.* When I'm meeting someone new, I like to meet for coffee. My goal is to show up and be excited about getting to know her rather than worrying what she might have heard about me or wondering if I'm impressing her. After we chat about mutual friends and favorite hobbies or foods, I then like to find out about her relationship with God. Here are some questions that you might find useful:

   • How long have you been coming to our church?
   • When did you start following Jesus?
   • Where have you seen God working in your life?
   • What have you been praying about lately?
   • Do you sense God putting any dreams in your heart?

   The goal is to see if you have a natural connection, which would include things like shared life experiences, hobbies you both enjoy, or the same stage in life. You don't need to be in the same place spiritually, but you'll need to listen to see if her spiritual journey is compatible with where you're at.

You don't have to answer all of these questions in one conversation. Let the conversation flow. If these questions go well and you'd like to meet again, go for it. If you don't feel a connection, you can simply let her know that you enjoyed your time together. It's always good to meet people!

A *special note*: If you've enjoyed attending the same Bible study or women's group for years with mostly the same group of ladies, it's good to temperature check yourself to prevent taking sisterhood for granted or to address any unhealthy behaviors. Here are some reflection questions to ask yourself or to begin a discussion with your group:

- Are group members internally focused (the "us four and no more" or sorority mentality), or are you involved in serving gospel-centered interests outside of the group?
- Do group sessions still focus on Jesus, the gospel, and spiritual challenge, or do group meetings sound more like political parties, social activism, self-help, or complaining sessions?
- Is the group a safe, patient environment for people to struggle with issues or question their beliefs?

15

CELEBRATING YOUR STRENGTH

GRATITUDE

It is always possible to be thankful for what is given rather than complain about what is not given. One or the other becomes a habit of life.

Elisabeth Elliot

"God, You did THIS!" That is the shout of celebration.

Celebration is recognizing the evidence of God's goodness and intentionally creating a moment around it. When was the last time you celebrated a moment or milestone in your life? I'm not talking about a birthday party or anniversary. I'm talking about celebrating God moments.

In a world where we're always rushing on to the next thing, celebration is pausing in our push toward progress and giving praise to God. This pause can look a lot of different ways, and we'll explore that later in the chapter. Right now, we need to talk about why celebration is as necessary in our lives as getting groceries or taking a shower. It's that life-giving for us!

For years, I've made it a practice to ask people how they plan to celebrate whenever they tell me about finishing a big project at work, persevering through a long season with a child, or tackling something tough like clearing out a parent's house. Most people ask me to repeat the question because celebration isn't something on their radar. Often their next response is a shrug followed by, "Um, I don't know."

It might be strange to think about celebration as a godly practice because it can be fun! Most of the time our attitude toward having to practice something is "Do I have to?" But what if I told you that celebration is motivation? It is! When you celebrate, you extend that "God, You did this!" moment so it becomes stored in your memory. Then, when you're going through tough seasons or fighting stress starters, you can tap into your celebration memories and replay your winning track record with God to boost your mood and attitude.

As we talk about the practice of celebration, let's focus on your practice of marking special moments that happen in your life. It's wonderful that you show up with your special dip or side dish for someone's birthday or anniversary. Celebration is easy when we think about hosting a party or buying gifts for others. But for the purpose of this chapter, let's keep the focus on you. Are you willing to celebrate you and what God has done in you or through you?

Have you ever been around a Christian woman who has led a women's event, won an award, or shared her testimony? When someone congratulates her, she will generally respond one of two ways: "Oh, it was all God" or "It wasn't just me." Those responses may reflect humility, but aren't they also missing the important ingredient of how God used that person—her time, talent, and treasure? Yes, God was at work, but He worked through a human body. Why is that so hard for Christian women to acknowledge and celebrate? I propose that not acknowledging and celebrating misses out on an opportunity to give God glory.

A journey to the mountaintop isn't complete once you reach the peak. The practice of celebration combines your accomplishment with the acknowledgment of God's involvement in that experience. This can happen privately and publicly.

Celebration can also look like coming back to life again. How many times has God miraculously breathed new life into the dry bones of your weariness or apathy? You can celebrate that! Some of us have seen God bring relationships, financial situations, or our health back to life, or we have seen Him bring our children back from the dead-end destinations that only He could turn around. You can celebrate that! If God has healed you from your broken past and lost dreams, that's cause for celebration.

If you don't stop and acknowledge God's presence and power in a meaningful way, there's the danger that you won't appreciate the totality of what He has done. You'll rob yourself of the full reflection of His faithfulness, His promises, and possibly even His miraculous hand in your life. The practice of intentional celebration intersects with our unending sources of stress and serves as a type of ballast that strengthens our resolve to endure and carry on.

Ready to party yet?

God is the original party planner. In Exodus 12, He provided instructions for how the Israelites were to gather and celebrate after they'd been freed from slavery. This tradition would become known as the Passover, and God told them to observe the occasion and celebrate each year.

The Israelites might have gotten a taste of such celebrations during the four hundred years they spent in Egypt, except they were never invited to the party. It's not hard to imagine that the labor for Pharaoh's celebrations came at the expense of the

Israelites and other enslaved people. I wonder how the Israelites received the good news that God wanted them to celebrate specific feasts throughout the year, only now they were guests of honor instead of forced labor.

In Leviticus 23 we read how God outlined instructions for the Israelites to celebrate seven festivals throughout the year:

> Give the following instructions to the people of Israel. These are the LORD's appointed festivals, which you are to proclaim as official days for holy assembly. (v. 2)

These celebrations were not limited to a few people who met certain requirements. God commanded that, just as everyone was to take part in the preparations, so everyone was to participate in the celebrations. As women, we're often the ones planning the celebrations for others. We'll spend hours scrolling Pinterest for ideas, recipes, decorations, and invitations, and we'll search for just the right cake or gift. In the process, we'll experience a swinging pendulum of emotions—from excitement to exhaustion, from anticipation to overwhelm. Many of us would like to put that kind of effort into doing something special for ourselves, but we won't because either we're too busy taking care of everyone else or, more likely, we look at our imperfections and decide that we don't deserve to celebrate ourselves.

Not only did God command the Israelites to practice celebration, but He instructed them to start and end their celebrations with Sabbath. He gave the people a day to rest up before they started their celebration. Of course, God's festivals included plenty of food, and that food had symbolic meaning. For example, during the Festival of Firstfruits, families would bring the first sheaf of grain from their harvest and offer it to God in thanksgiving for His provision. Music was also incorporated, as with the Feast of Trumpets in which trumpet blasts marked the end of the growing season. Like a party planner with a purpose, God designed each of the Old Testament festivals to foreshadow an event related to Jesus. For example, the Feast of Trumpets points ahead to the trumpets that will sound at Jesus's second coming.

How serious was God about these celebrations? Ten times in Leviticus 23 He refers to them as days for "holy assembly" or "sacred assembly." God wanted His people to view these celebrations as special times set apart from the events of their everyday lives. The Festival of Shelters was an eight-day celebration commemorating how God freed the Israelites from slavery in Egypt. He instructed them to "celebrate with joy before the LORD your God for seven days" (Lev. 23:40). God wanted His people to have a great time!

All I have to say is, sign me up! If you were brought up in a religious tradition that taught you to see God as austere and stern, reading about God's commands to celebrate should challenge you to learn more about God's heart and character.

My constant battle with overwhelm during my twenties and thirties made it hard for me to relax and enjoy any moment. I was so used to stress that I didn't know how to celebrate when I had the chance. I spent decades sabotaging celebrations in my life. If everything wasn't perfect or if I felt like I hadn't earned it, I couldn't or wouldn't allow myself to celebrate a special moment. There might be someone out there who was scarred by the sight of me melting down in the middle of the street on a beautiful day in Grand Cayman on my thirty-fifth birthday. I packed up my overwhelm and took it on vacation with me, and it nearly ruined my trip. If you witnessed that, my apologies. I'm better now.

We sabotage celebration when we load it down with expectations, prerequisites, and quid pro quos. Some of us see it as a trophy to be earned by those who are organized, focused, or worthy enough to get the job done well, or who have taken care of everyone else first. Some of us think we don't deserve celebration until we deem ourselves worthy. Maybe your hiccup isn't about whether you deserve the right to celebrate, but you withhold celebration until everything around you is settled or you've made sure to celebrate everyone else first. Perhaps you think that celebration is at the end of the rainbow and you can't have it a second sooner.

If you can relate and reading this has triggered some grief or guilt, close your eyes and take a deep breath. If you recognize that you've been resistant to celebration or have sabotaged celebration, are you willing to submit to God's way? If so, it's a new day! Celebration doesn't have to be perfect, but it can be precious if we embrace it. The whole point of this book is to learn new practices so that we can experience God's work of shalom wholeness within us.

Let's look at ways to incorporate the practice of celebration into our lives in a way that leads us into God's great wholeness and joy.

Gratitude and Praise

Gratitude and praise are the building blocks of celebration. Since celebration motivates us to keep trusting God and remembering His goodness, tap into gratitude and raise your spirits when you're feeling low. Psalm 100 is a popular praise psalm, and Eugene Peterson offers a highly relatable paraphrase in *The Message* that you can use as practical praise instruction:

> On your feet now—applaud GOD!
>   Bring a gift of laughter,
>   sing yourselves into his presence.
>
> Know this: GOD is God, and God, GOD.
>   He made us; we didn't make him.
>   We're his people, his well-tended sheep.

Enter with the password: "Thank you!"
Make yourselves at home, talking praise.
Thank him. Worship him.

For God is sheer beauty,
all-generous in love,
loyal always and ever.

Look at all the ways the psalmist lists that we can praise God, including singing, laughter, joy, and that all-important password: *thank you*. You can write out a gratitude list each day, use a gratitude app on your phone, or spend time in prayer giving thanks to God. The point of gratitude is not how you do it but that you do it. There's no way that you can overdo giving thanks to God.

During the earliest days of the COVID-19 pandemic, I felt all the stress starters because I was in a new season of life, my job was interrupted, and the future was uncertain. I started a gratitude jar by placing a two-quart jar and a stack of pre-cut scrapbooking paper on my dining room table. Whenever I walked by the table, I'd stop and write down something that I saw God doing in my life or another moment of gratitude. I did this for ninety days and the jar was full.

Two fun things happened during that exercise. First, it opened my eyes to how often God was blessing me. Second, as I watched that jar fill up, I was reminded of how good and generous God is to me. This is an exercise that you can do on your own or as a family. I saved mine as a time capsule to open in five years, and I'll celebrate those moments again!

Not only does gratitude give glory to God, but evidence supports that a regular practice of gratitude reduces stress. Studies have shown that people who keep a gratitude journal have 23 percent lower stress hormones and overall experience better quality of sleep, have stronger immune systems, and eat healthier.[1]

Gratitude gives us life and motivates us to keep turning toward God!

Me-and-God Celebrations

We often save celebration for big moments like birthdays, anniversaries, promotions, holidays, and graduations. But I want you to also include celebration times that are just between you and God. You can have so much fun with this!

Every time we pause to celebrate, we recognize that God is at work and we want to acknowledge that work, big or small. I'm a big fan of celebrating making it to the end of a long week. I've celebrated by getting down on my hands and knees and praising God for specific moments that He brought me through. When I see friends on social media who have landed a big account, made it through a scary medical test, or accomplished a goal, I'll text them a video message cheering them on and encouraging them to mark the moment by celebrating how God made it possible.

When I turn in a new book to my editor, I celebrate. Some might argue that I shouldn't celebrate until the book releases, but I disagree. It took a lot of prayer, perseverance, and struggle to get to that stage, and I want to give thanks to God for getting me there. It's a celebration between me and God. I may book a massage or take a long prayer walk. What makes this a me-and-God celebration is that I carve out time to give thanks to God for giving me the strength to complete that stage of the journey.

Pair celebration with other practices. For example, plan a special me-and-God celebration after you clean out your closet because eliminating the excess will simplify your decisions and reduce stress in the morning. Celebrate stepping out in obedience. If God prompts you to do something and you do it, offer up celebration as a praise to God.

Spiritual Milestones

Anytime someone takes a step with God is worth celebrating. When you or someone you know says yes to following Jesus, gets baptized, dedicates a child, graduates from Sunday school, or has an anniversary of joining their Bible study or small group, mark those moments with intentional celebration.

The size or scale doesn't matter but the moment does. I suggest borrowing from the pattern of celebration that God introduced in the Old Testament by incorporating food, singing, or playing worship songs in the background. Set aside at least a few minutes to openly give thanks to God. This could mean asking the person being celebrated to write out their story in advance and share it, or having a mentor, leader, or pastor say a few words about the person or their spiritual journey. Since we have technology at our disposal, capturing a photo of the person and a group photo of everyone who was part of that celebration would be a way to remind everyone of how God is still at work.

Cheer Others On

In Romans 12:15, Paul tells us to "be happy with those who are happy, and weep with those who weep." He instructs us to ride the ups and downs of life with other believers, including celebrating the things that they are celebrating.

Paul draws attention to the reality that we all face ups and downs in life. What a tragedy it would be if we faced them alone. What kind of witness would we have as believers if we didn't show up to celebrate each other? The Christian life is hard, but together we can find encouragement when we see God at work in a person's life and partake in that moment with them by taking time to hear and celebrate their story. Likewise, when pain and loss come, we can be there for people too. Those sad times remind us of how important it is to celebrate in the happy times.

At the end of this chapter, I include a practice to help you get started. But first I want to close by sharing how God brought a surprise celebration into my life and for once I didn't sabotage it.

For my last special birthday, my family threw me a surprise party. They spent months coordinating with each other on a secret Facebook page. My sister came to stay with me, using the truth-skirting story that since we were born three years and one day apart, she thought we should spend our birthdays together that year. I agreed and dismissed any questions I had about how she could get away from her busy job in Washington, DC.

Unbeknownst to me, my children and sister coordinated with friends and family to provide snacks, decorations, and even a deluxe gluten-free German chocolate cake. Invitations were sent far and wide, and even friends from high school RSVP'd.

Guests began to arrive that Friday evening. The party was supposed to start at 5:30 p.m. But I wasn't there.

I was at home in bed. Asleep.

The Monday of that week would have been my thirtieth wedding anniversary and had marked four years since the end of my marriage. It hadn't been an awful day, but it hadn't been easy either. I just wasn't in the mood to celebrate.

On Friday, the day of the party, I'd spent a sweaty afternoon at the zoo with my kids. I returned home hot and a hot mess from crying on and off throughout the day. At one point I told my youngest daughter, "I'm so glad that I didn't plan a party for myself." I found out later that she snuck off to send an SOS text to her siblings: *Mom's not okay.*

I climbed into bed at 3:30 that afternoon, still in my sweaty clothes. I pulled a bonnet on my head and got under my covers. When a Black woman pulls her bonnet on her head, that means she's done for the day, and don't bother talking her out of it.

My sister came into my room to nudge me awake. I found out later that it took her a few tries. She reminded me that my kids were waiting to take me out to dinner that night. The only thing that got me out of that bed was the knowledge that my kids were home and waiting for me. By that point it was 5:45.

I wiped off my face and told my sister that I wasn't doing my hair, and that I would change my shirt but not my pants. I laugh about that now.

Since I hadn't had a birthday party since I was twelve years old, you can imagine the stunned look on my face when I walked into the party at 6:15 and heard "SURPRISE!"

A decade earlier, I would have spent the entire evening interrogating family members to figure out how they'd worked so efficiently behind my back. I may have circulated the room and said things like, "I can't believe that they did this" or "Why did they go to all of this trouble for me?" But as I've learned how important celebration is to the heart of God and that the point of celebration is to take a moment to thank God, this time my heart was open to receive and enjoy the beautiful blessing that God bestowed on me. I could receive that generous gesture of love from my family and friends, and I could recognize God's comfort in surrounding me with support during a time when my heart was broken.

I hope that you take the practice of celebration as seriously as the other spiritual practices. Don't make the mistake of minimizing celebration just because it might include a party. Our circumstances aren't the reason we celebrate, God is. Celebration is good because celebration is from God.

Celebration makes space for us to look back across the waters of our Jordan Rivers and acknowledge that God brought us through. Just as God paused the Israelites on their way into the promised land and told them to set up the memorial stones, God created celebration to pause us so that we remember His power in our lives.

Celebrating as a Spiritual Practice

Daily Practice

- Give thanks to God for three ways that you saw Him at work in your life or three things that you're thankful for.
- Create a playlist with worship songs and play one per day as part of your celebration practice.

Weekly Practice

Ask a friend to join you in a weekly phone call or text to share and celebrate something that God has done or how you see God working in your lives.

Monthly or Annual Practice

On your calendar, write in the dates of spiritual milestones such as your date of salvation, baptism, anniversaries of ministry service, or participation in ministry moments like mission trips or outreach events.

Here are a few ideas of how to celebrate:

- Acknowledge the special day on social media by sharing your story and a photo of that day.
- Mark the moment at your Bible study or small group by sharing with them. A special dessert or shared meal could be an option because food makes celebrations fun!
- Celebrate privately with you and God by taking a walk to reflect and have a special time of worship.

16

NOW WHAT DO I DO?

By his divine power, God has given us everything we need
for living a godly life.

2 Peter 1:3

We've learned about ten spiritual practices and how to apply
them in our lives. I pray that now you're equipped, encour-
aged, and inspired to dive in. I also suspect that you might
be a little perplexed how these practices fit into the flow of
the circus that's already underway in your life. This chapter
serves as a next step and a road map to helping you figure
out how to integrate these spiritual practices in a way that
works for you.

You don't need to jump into all ten of these practices at once.
Depending on your temperament, you might be tempted to
believe that you can overcome your overwhelm by doing all of
them. That's not how this works. Spiritual practices are a way

for you to create space for God to transform you, not tools for you to DIY your spiritual growth.

Start Right Where You Are

If you've been struggling spiritually or you haven't engaged with God lately, don't let that stop you from beginning a spiritual practice. In fact, starting a new practice might be the jump start that you need to reconnect with God in a structured yet meaningful way. If you're already engaged in a practice, then incorporate some of the practical tips that I've shared to deepen your experience. If you're at the starting line, that's great!

You can count on God's promise in 2 Peter 1:3 that He will provide what you need to know Him, grow in Him, and experience all that He has promised. Even when you're tired, questioning, confused, struggling, or angry, you show up. God can handle it and He will help you.

Be Present, Not Perfect

One of my favorite slogans is "Just for today." The intent of this slogan is to remind us that we don't have to figure everything out all at once, nor should we place unreasonable anxieties or expectations on ourselves about the future. The focus is on doing what we can today.

Before you can engage in any spiritual practices, you need to be present. Be where your feet are in the moment. There will always be the next item on your to-do list, there will always be another errand to run, but when you are purposefully present for any practice, God has a way of shape-shifting time, space, and priorities so that whatever time you spend with Him multiplies your energy, strength, efficiency, and peace when you pick back up with your life. Spending time with God is never wasted time.

One Minute Can Make a Wonderful Difference

If you're feeling overwhelmed by all these practices or intimidated by certain practices, see below for one-minute versions of the spiritual practices that I created to encourage you. While it's true that the more room you make for God, the more you can receive from Him, it's also true that God can take a little and do a lot with it.

For those who are just starting and wondering if a one-minute practice can make a difference, here's what God says in Zechariah 4:10: "Do not despise these small beginnings, for the LORD rejoices to see the work begin."

Keep showing up and doing something to create space for you and God each day. Little bit by little bit you'll see His Spirit at work and you'll notice the growing presence of His peace within.

Picking Your Spiritual Practices Starter Pack

For those who wonder which practices to start with, I've created a starter pack combination of practices. This also includes a few prompts to help you choose your starting point.

As your experience with a practice grows, you can enjoy growing in the other practices as well.

STARTER PACK RECOMMENDATIONS AND ONE-MINUTE PRACTICES FOR THE FOUR DIFFERENT TYPES OF OVERWHELM

Overfunctioning
- Doing too much
- Difficulty saying no
- Feeling responsible for too much
- Inability to stop and rest
- Trying to satisfy too many or unreasonable expectations

Surrender

One-Minute Practice: Inhale and Release

If there is something in your path that you cannot fix, change, or control, it's an indicator that you need to release it to God. Take a deep breath, and as you exhale, breathe out, "God, I release this to Your care, Your control, and Your outcome."

Sabbath

One-Minute Practice

While Sabbath is a day set aside to rest with God, you can take a one-minute rest whenever you need to. Take that minute to enter the Breathing Room and practice one of those exercises, or close your eyes and listen to worship music.

Prayer

One-Minute Practice: "Here with Me" Prayer

Practicing God's presence throughout the day will be the energy boost that you need when things are intense. Here are a few one-minute prayers you can use to acknowledge God's presence:

- *God, I know that You are here with me right now.*
- *God, I know that You are with me and for me, and You will not fail me.*
- *Open my eyes, God, to where You are working right now.*

Celebration

One-Minute Practice

Spend one minute sitting and giving thanks to God for the gift of life and how He has provided for you.

Overthinking	Surrender
• Thinking too much about everything • Regularly second-guessing decisions • Anxiety over failure	*One-Minute Practice: Inhale and Release* If there is something in your path that you cannot fix, change, or control, it's an indicator that you need to release it to God. Take a deep breath, and as you exhale, breathe out, "God, I release this to Your care, Your control, and Your outcome." **Scripture** *One-Minute Practice* Either choose a favorite verse from this book or a favorite verse that you've heard before and read it aloud once. Close your eyes and take a deep breath. Then read it aloud again and meditate on it: • What does this verse remind you about God, His character, or His promises? • In what ways does this verse remind, encourage, or instruct you? **Simplicity** *One-Minute Practice* There are several practical ways to practice one-minute simplicity: • Look at your calendar or to-do list for the day and eliminate one errand, phone call, or task. • Challenge yourself to say no to an unnecessary obligation where you'd be tempted to say yes. • Look at one area where you have too many things and remove three items that you don't use, to create more space. **Celebration** Take a minute to walk around your home and lay your hand on possessions while giving thanks to God for His blessings.

Obsessing	Surrender
• Stuck on expecting a certain result or outcome • Inability to stop a certain behavior	*One-Minute Practice: Inhale and Release* If there is something in your path that you cannot fix, change, or control, it's an indicator that you need to release it to God. Take a deep breath, and as you exhale, breathe out, "God, I release this to Your care, Your control, and Your outcome." **Submission** *One-Minute Practice* When faced with a decision or a strong emotional tug, take one minute to practice submission by praying, "God, help me see what You want me to do and help me to be willing to do it." **Sacrifice** *One-Minute Practice* During the day, sacrifice a quick scroll on social media while you wait for an order, wait for someone to get into the car, or wait for a meeting to begin, and instead use that time to acknowledge God and give thanks for His presence in your life. **Celebration** *One-Minute Practice* Reflect on a time in life when God brought you through an unexpected event or hardship, and give thanks to Him. Note how that experience deepened your faith or made you stronger as a person.

Overloaded	Surrender
• Weighed down by guilt, shame, or problems of the past • Carrying others' expectations and problems	*One-Minute Practice: Inhale and Release* If there is something in your path that you cannot fix, change, or control, it's an indicator that you need to release it to God. Take a deep breath, and as you exhale, breathe out, "God, I release this to Your care, Your control, and Your outcome." **Self-Care** *One-Minute Practice* Set a timer and smile at yourself in the mirror for one minute while reminding yourself that God loves and cares for you and that you are worthy and valuable. **Sisterhood** *One-Minute Practice* Open up your text messages and pray for the person whose name appears at the top of the screen. If you have time, pray for the next person in the list. **Celebration** *One-Minute Practice* Remember one difficult moment from your past and give thanks to God that He brought you through it.

Set Yourself Up for Success

If you've chosen a set of practices that you'd like to start with, here are two more suggestions to equip you for long-term participation, even if you experience bumps or stops along the way.

1. Give Yourself a Star

While I discourage a legalistic approach to the spiritual practices, there's nothing wrong with creating a system to help you stay engaged or accountable. Just like the YouVersion Bible app includes check marks to note completed Bible readings and a digital counter to announce a daily streak, you can chart your commitment to the practices. Maybe it's simply marking an X on the calendar when you complete a certain practice. I like the suggestion in *Atomic Habits* where a stockbroker put 120 paper clips in a jar. Each time he made a phone call, he'd transfer one paper clip to a waiting empty jar. The instant gratification of seeing his progress kept him committed.[1] You can adapt that idea for whatever practice you're focused on that week.

2. Preplan Your Restarts

If you start a practice, plan in advance for how you'll restart if you get interrupted. Life happens. You go on vacation, a kid gets sick—lots of things can cause you to skip a day or a week. Don't give up! Preplan how you'll start again. I have an easy suggestion that you can apply to spiritual practices and even to other areas of your life.

Popular wisdom is that our natural motivation rises at the beginning of each month. So if your progress is interrupted for any reason, don't stew on why you stopped; check the calendar and make plans to restart on the first day of the new month.

How Will You Know If Your Practices Are Working?

You'll know. The tip-off will be a growing sense of peace you feel inside that sticks around even though your circumstances are still too much. Another tip-off is that you will sense a magnetic pull to keep creating space for God. The more you make room for God, the more you'll want to make room for Him. Keeping a journal is a great way for you to notice how your daily experience with life and God changes.

My prayer is that these spiritual practices become so natural to you that you won't even think of them as practices; rather, they will become well-worn paths you travel to meet and enjoy time with God.

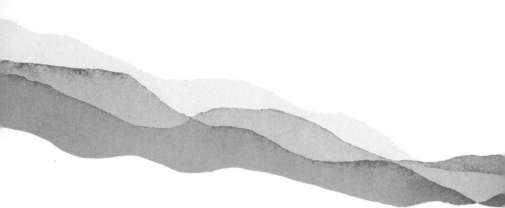

17

OVERCOMING SPIRITUAL OPPOSITION

ROMANS 8

And they have defeated him by the blood of the Lamb and
by their testimony.

Revelation 12:11

I hadn't planned this chapter when I first brainstormed this
book. I figured that I'd explain how stress and overwhelm work,
teach you the faith-deepening spiritual practices, equip you
with effective tools, and then send you on your way with Jesus.
Then I remembered that this book wasn't inspired by the spiritual practices per se but by my experience of God's incredible
peace, power, and faithfulness over years of relentless spiritual
opposition.

There were times when I was convinced that the fiery arrows
of the enemy were hitting me all day and night. I believed God

when He promised that no weapon would prosper (Isa. 54:17), but He never said anything about the weapons not causing pain. One such attack stripped me of my ability to speak for three days from the complete and utter overwhelm. I spent those days in my bed and on my knees silently praying and crying out to God. His gentle whisper came in the form of ten simple words that had the power to calm the deep sea of my overwhelm:

> The LORD himself will fight for you. Just stay calm. (Exod. 14:14)

Moses spoke those words to the Israelites after they had left Egypt and as Pharaoh's army was pursuing them to destroy them. When His people were faced with an enemy that was about to overpower them, God showed up and won the fight.

This is what God will do for you.

Deep in the underbelly of overwhelm is an enemy who doesn't want you to believe that God is faithful to His promises. In the cloud of chaos, our enemy lurks, planting questions of doubt in our minds. Rather than giving him more attention than he deserves, in this discussion let's focus our real attention on how God responds to spiritual opposition and what He instructs us to do.

> For we are not fighting against flesh-and-blood enemies, but against evil rulers and authorities of the unseen world, against mighty powers in this dark world, and against evil spirits in the heavenly places. (Eph. 6:12)

Author Priscilla Shirer describes what this looks like in the battle of overwhelm: "This is war. The fight of your life. A very real enemy has been strategizing and scheming against you, assaulting you, coming after your emotions, your mind, your man, your child, your future. In fact, he's doing it right now this very second."[1]

Right now some of you are saying, "Yes, that's exactly what's happening!" You have a sense that some of your overwhelm isn't happening because of your schedule or your choices but because for whatever reason there's been an escalation of spiritual attack in your life. Depending on how you react in survival mode, you may have tried a variety of scenarios to try to do your part to battle the enemy. To be clear, you cannot win a spiritual battle on your own. It's good to pray, but prayer without God's power will not win the battle. It's good to fast, but fasting without God's power cannot win the battle. God's not sitting in heaven waiting for you to pray a certain number of prayers or to live perfectly for a certain number of days before saying, "Okay, you did enough for me to fix this." The battle belongs to the Lord! God doesn't leave you in a situation a second longer than what serves His eternal purposes and your good.

We can't hurry God's eternal purpose, but we can learn how to discern what God wants us to do in seasons of spiritual opposition. We can take some of our cues from Jesus, who faced direct spiritual opposition from Satan after fasting for forty days and forty nights in the wilderness.

> Then Jesus was led by the Spirit into the wilderness to be tempted there by the devil. For forty days and forty nights he fasted and became very hungry. During that time the devil came and said, "If you are the Son of God, tell these stones to become loaves of bread." (Matt. 4:1–3)

In His humanity, Jesus was weak, and Satan knew this. It's the same for us in our overwhelm. When you're living in survival mode or you aren't deeply connected to God, Satan knows that he can move in and start messing with you or some of your plates and you'll melt down in fear or hopelessness.

Over the years, I've received countless emails from women who've gone through these seasons. I've heard from wives who feel abandoned. They see other women experiencing joy and blessing while their own marriage suffers from one crisis after the next. I've heard from mothers whose children have been diagnosed with chronic and rare diseases even though they were careful with their nutrition and care. The psalmist often lamented, "How long, God? How long?" and we can feel that way too.

In my own life, I recognized that sometimes I needed to be able to point to Satan stirring things up because it's much easier to be angry with Satan than to admit that I'm angry with God. But the reality is that God's Spirit led Jesus into the situation where He faced spiritual opposition. He did not leave Jesus alone in that place though. The Holy Spirit was with Jesus to guide and comfort. We are never alone when we face spiritual opposition. Remember, spiritual opposition isn't a punishment. It is Satan's attempt to get us to "curse God and die," much like Job's wife tempted him (Job 2:9). Right now, Satan wants you to be so angry with God for letting all of this happen that you turn away from God. At that point, Satan knows you are like a helpless animal and he can take you down much easier.

The best way for you to remember that God is with you in seasons of spiritual opposition is to keep making room in your life for God to show up. When Satan tempted Jesus to turn stones into loaves of bread, Jesus responded by saying, "No! The Scriptures say, 'People do not live by bread alone, but by every word that comes from the mouth of God'" (Matt. 4:4). Victory over the spiritual opposition we face begins when we arm ourselves with God's Word and position ourselves behind the power of God. The power is in the blood of Jesus—the power that forgives sin, breaks strongholds, and brings freedom—and that is the power we have each and every day. In Revelation 12, we're told that a day will come when the long battle will be over. At that point, we will not only stand in victory but live forever in the fullness of that victory. On that day when the final battle is won, we will testify to the power of Jesus's blood and tell the stories of how we overcame the obstacles and overwhelm in Jesus's name.

Until that day comes, we live in the promise that Jesus has overcome anything that the enemy can throw at us. Paul says, "If God is for us, who can ever be against us?" (Rom. 8:31). We are in a battle, but we are not defenseless. You are stronger than your stress when you remember this:

God is bigger than your biggest anxiety, problem, or fear of the future.

It might seem like the army of hell has been unleashed against you. Attacks on your faith, your family, your finances, your health, or your friendships stun you and send you to your knees praying, "God, what's going on here?" It's as if someone else is purposefully knocking down all your spinning plates, and you feel scared. As you're wondering what's going on, you may suspect that there is more occurring than what your human eyes can see.

Spiritual opposition feels scary because, while we may not understand it, we know it's real. In John 10:10, Jesus says that Satan's aim is to steal and kill and destroy. Priscilla Shirer talks about the specificity of spiritual opposition and why it feels so personal. She writes, "You may have noticed, the battles your enemy wages against you—especially the most acute, consistent ones—possess a personality to them, an intimate knowledge of who you are and the precise pressure points where you can most easily be taken down."[2] Spiritual opposition feels so personal because it is.

At the same time, God's protection for you is also personal. God never loses sight of you. Not for one single moment. You are more than a conqueror. Paul reminds us of God's power and how that same power breathes into each one of us:

> The Spirit of God, who raised Jesus from the dead, lives in you. And just as God raised Christ Jesus from the dead, he will give life to your mortal bodies by this same Spirit living within you. (Rom. 8:11)

Take a moment and internalize that truth: the same power that raised Jesus from the dead is the same power of the Holy Spirit that lives within you. This means that when you think you can't, God's Holy Spirit can. When you are confused, God's Spirit brings clarity. When you are overwhelmed, you can trust that you won't stay stuck because God's Spirit will make you an overcomer.

Nothing You Go Through Is Wasted

Romans 8:28 is one of those verses that can be misunderstood and create disappointment for believers who expect that God will wrap up the worst of life with a neat little bow on top. Paul writes,

> And we know that God causes everything to work together for the good of those who love God and are called according to his purpose for them.

But this verse is not a promise that God will bring a silver lining to heartbreaking situations. It is a reminder that God weaves all of what we experience into His eternal Big Picture plan for His eternal good.

In Hebrews 11 we read about the acts of faith done by various people in the Bible, including Noah, Abraham, Moses, Rahab, and many others. None of these people lived a perfect life, but when we read their stories, we see that good things eventually happened for many of them. Near the end of that chapter, however, we are told about a group of unnamed individuals who faced the worst that life has to offer—they were tortured, imprisoned, murdered, and oppressed. The author comments that these people were "too good for this world" (v. 38) and then says, "All these people earned a good reputation because of their faith, yet none of them received all that God had promised" (v. 39). These individuals didn't receive what we'd call a happy ending here on earth; however, they are right now living in the eternal peace and treasure of heaven.

It doesn't seem fair that those people suffered for God and met difficult ends, yet their stories bolster our faith when we read about them today. In the same way, people may not know your name or the story of how you survived difficult, devastating, or unthinkable circumstances, but God will weave your story into what He is doing and other people will become stronger because of the example of your faith.

As an author, I'm honored to receive emails and meet readers at events who tell me how my sharing my stories around anxiety, our family's addiction crisis, and letting go of control has helped them. But you don't have to write a book or be a public speaker. As you serve in your local church, build sisterhood with other women, and allow God to use you, you can be sure that He will use your life and your faith in ways far beyond what you could ever ask or imagine for His glory.

Your Circumstances Are Not the Measure of God's Love for You

At one point in Paul's story, he was stuck in prison for two years. He was kept under guard in Caesarea and even had an opportunity to share the gospel with the Roman governor Felix and his wife Drusilla (Acts 23:34–35; 24:24–27). Yet, Paul remained a captive in a cell, his future uncertain.

Shortly before his imprisonment, Paul wrote the following words from Romans 8. Notice all of the difficult circumstances he lists.

Can anything ever separate us from Christ's love? Does it mean he no longer loves us if we have trouble or calamity, or are persecuted, or hungry, or destitute, or in danger, or threatened with death? (As the Scriptures say, "For your sake we are killed every day; we are being slaughtered like sheep.") No, despite all these things, overwhelming victory is ours through Christ, who loved us. (vv. 35–37)

Paul reminds us that our circumstances, especially the stressful ones, shouldn't shake our confidence in God's love for us. When you're about ready to pull your hair out because so much is coming at you all at once, Satan would love for you to believe that God has abandoned you or rejected you, but that isn't true.

Let yourself linger on these words from Romans 8:35–37. There is strength in love. When you remember that God's love for you is constant, that knowledge will hold you up in the hardest of times. It's common for us to question God's love when we face the conditions that Paul writes about, but I love how he reminds us that it doesn't matter what we face—we are loved through it all.

Seek Refuge and Fill In Footholds

Whether you face spiritual opposition or the overwhelm that comes because of living in a broken world, you can run to God for refuge and fill in any footholds that the devil could try to use against you.

Refuge is a place of safety from a storm or an attack. God is your place of safety. There's no need to put off running to God because you're trying to figure out what's going on in your life. Sometimes, you may want to first see if the situation is just a small problem and handle it yourself, thinking you'll only turn it over to God if it's a big problem. In any storm or upheaval of life, big or small, turn it all over to God. You never know when a little situation will blow up into a big one.

In the classic movie *Twister*, Helen Hunt and Bill Paxton play Jo and Bill Harding, storm chasers who are driven by their own personal tragedies as they attempt to pilot a new piece of tornado detection equipment in an effort to save lives. In one scene, we see them racing through cornfields toward a tornado so that they can set up their device ahead of a rival team of storm chasers. Their rivals take a shortcut down a country road that appears to give them an advantage, but just then the radar shows a shift in the storm's direction. Jo and Bill hail their foes on the radio, pleading with them to change course. But the other team is so giddy at their apparent victory that they refuse to listen. They don't see the danger until it's too late. Their truck is swept up into the tornado and their lives are lost.[3]

It's easy to think you can handle spiritual battles on your own, but the battles are layered, complex, and without a doubt far over your head. You don't have what it takes to battle the enemy without the power of God. Give it all—the battle, the struggle, the overwhelm—to God from the very beginning.

Don't give the enemy a foothold in your life! A foothold is an opening from which someone can dig in and advance. We give Satan footholds when we question God's love or faithfulness, when we ignore God's leadings, or when we're disobedient. Not only does our initial act create a foothold, but the results of our action can create more footholds. Satan will insert himself into each one of those footholds and fill them with lies, temptation, and discouragement to make it even harder for you to live by faith. The spiritual practices in this book are foothold fillers. Each one strengthens your foundation of faith, making you stronger and proving that what was meant for evil, God used for good (Gen. 50:20).

IN CASE OF EMERGENCY

We can rejoice, too, when we run into problems and trials, for we know that they help us develop endurance. And endurance develops strength of character, and character strengthens our confident hope of salvation.

Romans 5:3–4

Maybe right now your life feels like an emergency. You need straightforward help, and you need it fast. When a situation is going downhill and you can't stop it, what do you need to remember about God before you try to handle it yourself at the expense of stressing out or getting in God's way? Below I've listed some quick hits or slogans for you to keep in mind or say out loud to yourself. While I've matched them with each of the ten spiritual practices, they are not a substitute for doing the deep and daily work of the Breathing Room exercises and other spiritual practices. Don't rob yourself of that time with God.

Surrender: *The answers will come.*

Sabbath: *Take a break before you break.*

Prayer: *Pray first.*

Scripture: *God's wisdom is better than yours.*

Simplicity: *Do all that you can but not more than you should.*

Self-Care: *On your worst days, treat yourself the best.*

Submission: *Let God lead.*

Sacrifice: *Whatever you give up for God will be for your good.*

Sisterhood: *Who can you call right now?*

Celebration: *What can you be grateful for in this moment?*

PRAYER FOR OVERCOMERS

One day, we'll say goodbye to overwhelm, anxiety, stress, and heartache. The Bible tells us, "He will wipe every tear from their eyes, and there will be no more death or sorrow or crying or pain. All of these things will be gone forever" (Rev. 21:4). Hallelujah! Oh, how we wait for that day!

But for today, we live in this world. We still need God's help.

It's been my practice to end my books and Bible studies with a final prayer for you, the reader. My hope is that this prayer stays with you in your battle against overwhelm long after you put this book on your shelf.

May God's grace and peace go before you,
May His strength and mercy meet you,
And may you never, ever forget . . .
God is with you.
　God is for you.
　God will never fail you.
God sees beyond what you can see.
God can carry what you can't.
God who IS the way when you can't see your way.
God who promised His presence.
　God will provide for you.
God will anchor you.
God will always love you.
In Jesus's name, amen.

ACKNOWLEDGMENTS

Kids and bonus in-law kids, thank you for loving me as I journeyed through what I wrote about in this book. I'm grateful and blessed to be your mom.

To my family and friends who prayed for me through long challenging years, may God bless you for holding me up and helping me hold on during the tough parts of life.

To CedarCreek Church, lead pastor Ben Snyder, and our amazing staff team. My friends, thank you for being a faithful church. You continue to inspire me to grow in my own walk with God.

Many thanks to my Books & Such agent, Janet Grant, who spent weeks planning and praying with me because this project would require a lot of personal sacrifice.

Thank you to Andrea Doering and the Revell team for welcoming me with enthusiasm and partnering with me on this book and Bible study.

Finally, I'm grateful to God who has graciously restored and redeemed far beyond what I could have ever asked or imagined.

NOTES

Chapter 1 Give Me a Break

1. Collins Dictionary, s.v. "overwhelm," accessed July 10, 2023, https://www.collinsdictionary.com/us/dictionary/english/overwhelm.

2. HealthyGamerGG, "If You're Feeling Overwhelmed, Watch This," YouTube video, accessed June 20, 2023, https://youtu.be/7VfSCQnGfk4.

3. Barb Roose, *Winning the Worry Battle: Life Lessons from the Book of Joshua* (Nashville: Abingdon, 2018), 21.

Chapter 2 Too Stressed to Be Blessed

1. Daniel Goleman, *Emotional Intelligence: Why It Can Matter More Than IQ* (New York: Bantam, 2005), 52.

2. Goleman, *Emotional Intelligence*, 14.

3. William Backus, *Learning to Tell Myself the Truth: A Six-Week Guide to Freedom from Anger, Anxiety, Depression and Perfectionism* (Minneapolis: Bethany House, 1994), 9.

Chapter 3 Get Off the Cross, Honey, Somebody Needs the Wood

1. N. T. Wright, *Paul: A Biography* (New York: HarperCollins, 2018), 63.

2. *Straight Talk*, directed by Barnet Kellman (Los Angeles: Hollywood Pictures, 1992).

3. Emily Nagoski and Amelia Nagoski, *Burnout: The Secret to Unlocking the Stress Code* (New York: Ballatine, 2019), 62.

Chapter 4 Seeing God's Big Picture beyond Stress

1. Moyer Hubbard, "2 Corinthians," *Zondervan Illustrated Bible Backgrounds Commentary*, ed. Clinton E. Arnold, vol. 3, *Romans to Philemon* (Grand Rapids: Zondervan, 2002), 253.

2. Chip Dodd, *The Voice of the Heart: A Call to Full Living*, 2nd ed. (Nashville: Sage Hill, 2014), 52.

3. *Strong's Concordance*, s.v. "8615. *tiqvah*," Bible Hub, accessed October 27, 2023, https://biblehub.com/hebrew/8615.htm.

Chapter 5 Stronger than Stress

1. "New Report Finds a Lack of Culturally Appropriate Self-Care Tools and Resources Is Impacting Black Women," Businesswire, June 26, 2023, https://www.businesswire.com/news/home/20230626949581/en/New-Report-Finds-a-Lack-of-Culturally-Appropriate-Self-Care-Tools-and-Resources-is-Impacting-Black-Women.

2. Noam Shpancer, "What Doesn't Kill You Makes You Weaker," *Psychology Today*, August 21, 2010, https://www.psychologytoday.com/us/blog/insight-therapy/201008/what-doesnt-kill-you-makes-you-weaker.

3. Mary Oliver, "Have You Ever Tried to Enter the Long Black Branches?," *West Wind: Poems and Prose Poems* (New York: Houghton Mifflin, 1997), 62.

4. Curt Thompson, *Anatomy of the Soul: Surprising Connections between Neuroscience and Spiritual Practices That Can Transform Your Life and Relationships* (Carol Stream, IL: Tyndale Momentum, 2010), 94.

5. Bittersweetgallery, "Week 1 of 52 PEACE IN THE MIDST OF THE STORM," YouTube, January 4, 2021, https://youtu.be/pGdIVgbD1U0.

6. Meghan Bartels, "What to Do When You Can't Fall Asleep May Surprise You," *Scientific American*, July 5, 2023, https://www.scientificamerican.com/article/what-to-do-when-you-cant-fall-asleep-may-surprise-you/.

7. *Strong's Concordance*, s.v. "1515. *eiréné*," Bible Hub, accessed July 13, 2023, https://biblehub.com/greek/1515.htm.

8. *Hidden Figures*, directed by Theodore Melfi (Fox 2000 Pictures, 2016).

Chapter 6 God, I Can't but You Can, So I Will Let You

1. Barb Roose, *Surrendered: Letting Go and Living Like Jesus* (Nashville: Abingdon, 2020), 37.

2. Richard J. Foster, *Celebration of Discipline*, 25th anniversary ed. (New York: HarperCollins, 1998), 30–31.

Chapter 7 Letting God Work While You Rest

1. Tiffany Shlain, *24/6: The Power of Unplugging One Day a Week* (New York: Gallery Books/Simon & Schuster, Inc. 2019), 24.

2. Ronald F. Youngblood, *Nelson's Illustrated Bible Dictionary: New and Enhanced Edition* (Nashville: Thomas Nelson, 2014), 1002.

3. Rebekah Lyons, *Rhythms of Renewal: Trading Stress and Anxiety for a Life of Peace and Purpose* (Grand Rapids: Zondervan, 2019), 74.

4. Since many Christians associate Sabbath with Sunday and football is played on Sunday, ESPN seemed like a meaningful acronym to work with here. For the record, I don't watch football on Sunday—or any day.

5. Shlain, *24/6*, 70–72.

6. S. P. Carter, K. Greenberg, and M. S. Walker, "Should Professors Ban Laptops? How classroom computer use affects student learning," *Education Next* 17, no. 4 (2017): 68–74.

Chapter 8 Talking to God

1. Charles Stanley, *How to Listen to God* (Nashville: Thomas Nelson, 1985), 14.

2. Ironically, while working as a drug rep, I argued with my own doctor at one point when he suggested that I needed to take an antidepressant because overwhelm and anxiety were running (and also ruining) my life. I argued that prayer should be enough. I was wrong. God used prayer plus counseling and medicine to bring healing into my life.

3. Goleman, *Emotional Intelligence*, 60.

4. Max Lucado, *Before Amen: The Power of Simple Prayer* (Nashville: Thomas Nelson, 2014), 19.

5. James Clear, *Atomic Habits: An Easy & Proven Way to Build Good Habits & Break Bad Ones* (New York: Avery Books, 2018), 31–33.

6. Priscilla Shirer, *Fervent: A Woman's Battle Plan for Serious, Specific and Strategic Prayer* (Nashville: B&H, 2015), 14.

Chapter 9 God Promised It, I Believe It

1. Adam Macinnis, "Report: 26 Million Americans Stop Reading Their Bible Regularly During COVID-19," *Christianity Today*, April 20, 2022, https://www.christianitytoday.com/news/2022/april/state-of-bible-reading-decline-report-26-million.html.

2. John Donovan, "How Atlanta Became the World's Busiest Airport, Again," HowStuffWorks, updated June 9, 2023, https://science.howstuffworks.com/transport/flight/modern/atlanta-worlds-busiest-airport.htm.

3. Nick Huss, "How Many Websites Are There in the World?," Siteefy.com, July 11, 2023, https://siteefy.com/how-many-websites-are-there/#How-Many-Webpages-Are-There.

Chapter 10 Decluttering the Yeses

1. Microsoft, "Introducing Microsoft To-Do," accessed July 19, 2023, https://www.youtube.com/watch?v=6k3_T84z5Ds.3.

2. Quoted in Sara Berg, "What Doctors Wish Patients Knew about Decision Fatigue," American Medical Association, November 19, 2021, https://www.ama-assn.org/delivering-care/public-health/what-doctors-wish-patients-knew-about-decision-fatigue.

3. "Home Organization Is Major Source of Stress for Americans, Survey Finds," *HuffPost*, May 22, 2013, https://www.huffpost.com/entry/home-orga nization-stress-survey_n_3308575.

Chapter 11 Taking Care of You

1. Christine Miserandino, "The Spoon Theory," ButYouDontLookSick .com, accessed December 19, 2023, https://butyoudontlooksick.com/articles /written-by-christine/the-spoon-theory/.

2. Institute of Medicine (US) Committee on Sleep Medicine and Research, "Extent and Health Consequences of Chronic Sleep Loss and Sleep Disorders," in *Sleep Disorders and Sleep Deprivation: An Unmet Public Health Problem*, ed. H. R. Colten and B. M. Altevogt (Washington, DC: National Academies Press, 2006), https://www.ncbi.nlm.nih.gov/books/NBK19961/.

3. Joni Eareckson Tada, "Cross Habits," JoniAndFriends.org, August 17, 2017, https://joniandfriends.org/4-minute-radio-program/cross-habits-2/.

Chapter 13 Giving Up for God's Holy Good

1. Quoted in Fred Zaspel, "The Theology of Sacrifice," The Gospel Coalition, accessed December 19, 2023, https://www.thegospelcoalition.org/essay /the-theology-of-sacrifice/.

2. Foster, *Celebration of Discipline*, 55.

3. Mahesh Chavda, *The Hidden Power of Prayer and Fasting* (Shippensburg, PA: Destiny Image, 2007), 147.

4. Joe DeCena, keynote address, CEO Spartan Races, EPIC Leadership Summit, Toledo, Ohio, November 9, 2017.

Chapter 14 Lean On Me

1. Brené Brown, *Daring Greatly: How the Courage to Be Vulnerable Transforms the Way We Live, Love, Parent, and Lead* (New York: Penguin Random House, 2012), 8.

2. Amanda Seitz, "Loneliness Poses Risk as Deadly as Smoking: Surgeon General," AP News, May 2, 2023, https://apnews.com/article/surgeon -general-loneliness-334450f7bb5a77e88d8085b178340e19, accessed May 3, 2023.

Chapter 15 Celebrating Your Strength

1. Lauren Dunn, "Be Thankful: Science Says Gratitude Is Good for Your Health," *Today*, updated November 24, 2021, https://www.today.com/health /be-thankful-science-says-gratitude-good-your-health-t58256.

Chapter 16 Now What Do I Do?

1. Clear, *Atomic Habits*, 195.

Chapter 17 Overcoming Spiritual Opposition

1. Shirer, *Fervent*, 2.
2. Shirer, *Fervent*, 6.
3. *Twister*, directed by Jan de Bont (Warner Bros., 1996).

BARB ROOSE is an author, a speaker at national women's conferences, and a regular contributor to (in)courage, Crosswalk, and iBelieve. She has written five Bible studies and four books and writes a weekly Happy Monday devotional. Barb serves as a teaching pastor at her home church with over 6,000 in weekly attendance. The proud mother of three adult kids, Barb loves reading and walking. Whenever possible, she prefers to eat dessert first.

Connect with Barb:

BarbRoose.com

 @barbararoose

@barbroose

AN INTERACTIVE BIBLE STUDY
TO HELP YOU OVERCOME OVERWHELM
WITH GOD'S PEACE

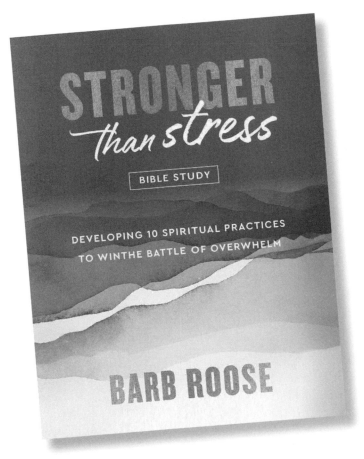

Stronger than Stress Bible Study offers 10 spiritual practices to help you overcome daily overwhelm with God's peace and strength. Learn from the life and teachings of the apostle Paul as you dive deeper into just how to make chronic stress and overwhelm a thing of the past by applying each practice to your life.